Dirty Dancing at the Prom

And Other Challenges Christian Teens Face

How Parents Can Help

Barbara Curtis

Beacon Hill Press of Kansas City
Kansas City, Missouri

Copyright 2005
by Barbara Curtis and Beacon Hill Press of Kansas City

ISBN 083-412-1859

Printed in the
United States of America

Cover Design: Brandon R. Hill

Library of Congress Cataloging-in-Publication Data

Curtis, Barbara, 1948–
    Dirty dancing at the prom and other challenges Christian teens face : how parents can help / Barbara Curtis.
        p. cm.
    ISBN 0-8341-2185-9 (pbk.)
    1. Parenting—Religious aspects—Christianity. 2. Parent and teenager—Religious aspects—Christianity. I. Title.

    BV4529.C86 2005
    248.8'45—dc22
                                                    2005012624

10 9 8 7 6 5 4 3 2 1

Contents

Introduction
The Secret Life of Teens

"What about the prom?"

Ben had just come home from rugby practice, leaving an unfortunate trail of mud in his wake, and was foraging for something substantial to eat. Even though it was getting close to six, I was avoiding the cautions about not spoiling his appetite. With a couple of testosterone-packed hours behind him and his six-foot-something frame, he could eat a full meal and still be hungry for dinner, I figured.

It was April, and the end of Ben's high school years was rolling out before us like a red carpet—so much to celebrate as he prepared himself for graduation and college. Recently he had been paying a lot of attention to a very special girl who had first caught his eye in study hall last year. I fully expected he would be asking her to the junior-senior prom, so I was surprised when Ben left my question hanging in the air.

"What about the prom?" I asked again.

"What about it?"

"Well, are you going to take Anna?"

"No."

"Really?" *Who else could he possibly want to ask?* I wondered.

"I'm not going to the prom." Ben said.

Did my jaw drop? I mean, I missed my own prom because I was too nerdy to rate a date. Why would a comfortably popular guy like Ben purposely miss his own?

"And I'm not going either," chimed in Zach—a year behind Ben in school and behind coming in because he had remembered to ditch his muddy clothes at the back door.

"And even if I did go, I would never take a girl like Anna," Ben said emphatically.

"But why?"

"She's too nice."

Too nice for what Ben knew would go on at prom, based on his homecoming dance experience the previous fall. As he began to elaborate, my dinner prep ground to a halt. The landscape seemed to shift in a Toto-we're-not-in-Kansas-anymore kind of way. Territory that I thought was familiar morphed into the strange and fantastic. Clearly, today's school dances were not at all the school dances parents remember.

Here's how kids I later interviewed described their school dances:

Joel, a northern Virginia senior who enjoys the dances: "I'm offended by the dancing and lack of respect for the teachers, but other than that, they're fine. Dancing includes the feeling of the opposite sex in all private areas, grinding, and gays dancing, making out, and kissing together."

Joshua—same region, different high school—says of school dances, "They're fun, and yes, they can be vulgar. My freshman year I looked over, and this guy and girl were acting like they were actually having sex. I saw that happen just that one time, and I haven't seen it since."

Well, thank goodness for that!

Still, most parents would probably be shocked by what goes on with just a couple layers of clothes in between.

It's called freak dancing, or "freaking," and includes boys grinding against girls as well as lines of kids similar to old-fashioned conga lines, except that everyone is gyrating tightly up against each other.

When I asked Ben and, later on, other kids the obvious question "What about the chaperones?" they explained that the dirtiest dancing wasn't on the fringes but actually in the center, like a ground zero on the dance floor, with layers of more modest dancing forming a buffer between the exhibitionists and the principal, teachers, and chaperones.

At Ben's school, according to student reports, the adults

were fairly content with this situation, clinging to the fringes themselves, avoiding confrontation. It helped enormously that the lights were off. As one chaperone reported, whenever the lights are turned up it's like flipping on a switch in a dark room and seeing the cockroaches running to hide.

The music played is usually hip-hop. In a small concession to decency, some schools use versions with offensive words bleeped out. At our local high school the result of this well-intentioned censorship was that the grinders on the dance floor filled in the blanks by yelling the expletives together.

Despite the prohibitions against alcohol and often the presence of police or security officers, kids I interviewed reported seeing kids drunk or stoned.

It was months later that I gathered these and hundreds of comments from kids across the country, after the dust settled and after I was asked to consider writing a book for parents to accomplish the following:

- to present a realistic picture of challenges faced by today's teens;
- to equip parents to empower their teens to meet those challenges.

When I say "after the dust settled," it's because for a few months before and after prom, there was what you might call "a whole lot of shaking going on"—and I don't mean on the dance floor.

It seems that some of the kids themselves had become fed up with the prom status quo: the status quo being not only a lack of respect and self-control on the part of the kids but also a lack of leadership and intervention by the adults.

Many, like Ben, simply decided not to go.

But Ben's friend, Christian, then a junior, decided to do something more. He hired a band and a hall—decorated with the help of friends—and for $10 a ticket offered his "Ante-Prom," held the night before and featuring swing music, optional costumes, good company, and unembarrassing fun.

Like many kids, Christian was turned off by the freak dancing at prom. But he also objected to the high cost of the evening, with tickets priced at $100 to cover the costs of the fancy hotel, plus tux, flowers, dinner, and the increasingly de rigueur limo service.

I, too, felt called to do something more. I wrote to the principal about the problems but received no answer. I wrote to the school board and the administration, only to be stonewalled: "Our high school has a wonderful reputation. Nothing like that could possibly happen there," I was told.

So I wrote a column for our local paper, not mentioning any particular school, but alerting parents to the problem of freak dancing, which had shut down school dances across the country.

Time for a Fresh Look at the Prom

Maybe it's time proms carried warning labels. As it is, most parents must be clueless about what goes on there.

Curious when my own sons and many of their friends said they weren't going to prom, I started asking questions. It seems that after one too many dances dominated by freak dancing—that is, dancing similar to what was once known as foreplay—they had just decided "Enough is enough."

A little research revealed that "freaking" has shut down dances in school districts across the country. Or forced school districts to forge written policies about what is appropriate behavior at school dances.

It's not just the kids who are to blame, but adults who dropped the ball in setting clear limits when freak dancing first reared its ugly head. Many parents would probably be shocked to see their normally well-mannered kids—who looked like Prince Charming and Cinderella in the pre-prom pictures—dancing a few hours later like an MTV nightmare.

See, the prom isn't like you and I remember it. It's a very dark room with hip-hop and rap music spewing obscenities and degrading stuff about women while kids get down and dirty. Reminds me of that joke about a certain denomination that didn't allow sex because it might lead to dancing.

Except it's more sad than funny. Make no mistake: while some girls enjoy this kind of exhibitionism, there are some basically nice girls who are just giving in to peer pressure or pressure from their dates. Talk about buyer's remorse—I'll bet a lot of them feel pretty bad about themselves the next morning.

Where are the chaperones? Good question. Loudoun requires one administrator, four teachers, and two parents at each dance. But remember, it's dark, dark, dark, and they can hang out on the sidelines, not seeing what they don't want to see. Besides, many are of the persuasion that "this is just what the kids are doing," "it's good for them to 'cut loose,'" "our parents didn't like the way we danced," etc.

I'm not buying this. Especially when even science is surprising us with new information about the immaturity of the teenage brain, with frontal lobes—the part responsible for decision-making—the last to develop, way after high school (<http://www.usaweekend.com/03_issues/030518/030518teenbrain.html>) While in calm situations, teenagers can rationalize as well as adults, under pressure or stress—especially that driven by hormones—they just can't cope.

Which is why we need to still be involved in setting limits and guiding our children through these foundational years. Laissez-faire parenting might have been an option a generation ago, but I can't see it today. Not when our kids face a daily barrage of downright dangerous messages.

Don't get me wrong—it's a free country and if some parents are cool with their kids freak dancing—well, throw them a party and let them grind away.

But keep public school dances inclusive. Let this be the last year some of our best and brightest walk away from prom.

—*Loudon Times-Mirror,* April 21, 2004

How in the world did we get here? Most parents probably remember proms in school gyms transformed with decorations galore. Ben's and Christian's school prom was held at a hotel 35 minutes from home. Many kids rented rooms and drank the night away. Though technically the school didn't condone kids having sex after the prom, the very fact that the prom was held at a hotel increased the likelihood.

This was exactly the sort of laissez-faire approach my husband, Tripp, and I had hoped to leave behind when we moved the year before from northern California to Virginia seeking a cultural milieu more compatible with our family's values, which had changed dramatically 17 years before when we became believers.

Before that, we had been laissez-faire ourselves, with no moral compass to guide us, just following the crowd. My daughter, Samantha, had attended her prom with her childhood sweetheart, Kip, and they had stayed at the hotel on the pretense of girls spending the night together in one room and boys in another.

I know what it's like to assume your kids are telling the truth when they're not. I also know what it's like to overlook the obvious. Shortly after the prom and graduation, Tripp and I, as well as Samantha and Kip, became Christians, and they confessed they had lied to us.

But our sin as parents was this: choosing to ignore the all-too-clear red flags of prom night, we opened the door to temptation.

But before I had a relationship with God, deluding myself about reality was easy.

On the other hand, becoming a Christian was like a light suddenly being turned on in a room we didn't even know was dark. As though—to borrow from Plato—Tripp and I had been watching shadows in an underground cave, thinking they were real, when someone had taken our hands and guided us up into the sunlight to see the true world.

Now, with our family built on God's foundation, the guidance of the Bible, and the influence of the Holy Spirit, everything we thought we knew was up for grabs. We began to see the error of our parenting ways.

Good thing too! Samantha was our oldest, and there were then 5 coming up behind. Eventually there would be 12. If anyone ever needed to become parenting experts, it was Tripp and me. Otherwise we would never have made it.

When we looked back over our family histories, there was nary a Christian in sight (except for one great uncle of Tripp's, a missionary now in his 90s). Recognizing our unique opportunity to change the legacy of our family, we poured a lot into our parenting, trying our best to live up to Deut. 11:19:

> *Teach* [the words of scripture] *to your children, talking about them when you sit at home and when you walk along the road, when you lie down and when you get up.*

We never took for granted that going to Sunday School or participating in church youth activities would secure our children's faith. We knew it had to be part of our everyday lives. I home-schooled our kids for the early years, which meant reading the Bible and singing hymns every day. I believe it was because of this early, intense bonding that when they were teens my kids told me everything, everything that was going on in their lives.

So now Ben (our fifth), facing his prom, didn't hesitate to tell me why he didn't want to go. In the 17 years since Samantha's and Kip's prom, it wasn't just Tripp and me that had changed. The world had changed as well.

And so, one simple question led me into a much more complicated world than I expected—one in which most parents are clueless, either because their children don't tell them or because—as Tripp and me with Samantha's prom—they would just rather not know.

Hence the title of this introduction, "The Secret Life of Teens."

In addition, one simple question lit a fuse and began the

countdown as the status quo of dances in all our county schools was due for an explosion. How the kids themselves—under the leadership of Ben's friend, Christian—stepped into the adult leadership vacuum to get things back on track will be discussed in a future chapter.

Finally, one simple question began a conversation I took beyond the kids I knew to teens across the country so that what was becoming more and more "the secret life of teens" might be revealed to parents in a way that would not only inform them about the way things really are for teens today but also equip and empower them to help their kids meet the challenges they face when it comes to dirty dancing at the prom and in every aspect of their everyday lives.

Self-esteem

My first question to the teens in one of my focus groups got the ball rolling.

Question: What's it like to walk down the hall of a high school today? What difficulties do you face each day?

Kristen, a college freshman from a small town in South Carolina, describes her high school experience: "Walking down the hall at my high school can be somewhat intimidating. If you bump into the wrong person, he or she will pick a fight with you, and according to our school rules, you have to just stand there and take it until a teacher or administrator pulls the person off of you. You get dirty looks, with varying degrees of violence or sexuality accompanying them. A lot of the freshmen are scared out of their minds and don't know how or who to ask for help."

Joel, a senior from Loudoun County in northern Virginia, notes, "Many groups of kids standing around in the hallway scream or yell profanities or sexual innuendos that the teachers themselves don't even understand, but all the students do."

Josh, a senior from Waynesboro, North Carolina, says, "You see all kinds of things in the hallways. I've seen people taking speed and using other drugs. Every once in a while, a fight breaks out."

Rachel (pseudonym), now homeschooled, comments, "When I went to public high school, I got looks from people I knew were Christians. They looked at me like I was strange, asked me sarcastically if I think I'm perfect and ridiculed me for wanting to be a virgin until I get married. I also heard a lot of bad, inappropriate conversations."

Brandon, a senior from Marin County, California, said, "My friends see my faith as a type of oddity. I don't believe they understand the full scope of what a relationship with Christ means. They think it is an oppressive, intolerant belief system that has gotten lost in the crowd of more modern and accepting belief systems. They think Christianity is outdated. I'm known as one of the few conservative, Christian students. I feel much more confident now, but at times—especially in the beginning of high school—it was intimidating and lonely."

Most parents would probably be surprised by these e-mail responses—just a few of the many I received from teens across the country—that reveal how stressful changing classes in a suburban high school can be for today's teens.

I was stunned at my first glimpses into the real world of teens when my editors kicked off this book by flying me to Kansas City to meet with a focus group of high school and first-year college students—all committed Christians, half with public school and half with Christian school experience.

Not that Christian school students are completely spared the moral challenges faced by their public school peers. Rick, a football player any girl would call a "hottie," said of his Christian school years, "Even there, it's not totally easy to just follow God 100 percent. Not all your friends are going to be Christians."

Still, he acknowledges it's worse in the public school he now attends: "In the locker room, it's just horrible what you hear. You want those guys to like you, but at the same time you don't want to go out and do what they do. Like a lot of the guys go to the strip clubs and stuff. 'Hey, Rick—you wanna go?' You want to be friends with the guys, but then if you go, you totally ruin your example for God. You can't witness to them after that, because you're then just like one of them. You can't do what they do—you've just got to be an example."

And Joanna, an exceptionally pretty blond of 16, had these words to describe the scene in her Midwest high school: "Walking down the halls you see gay people in the corner making out, and you see groups—the druggies, the freaks, you know. You just feel, like, really alone, like there's no one else that's like you in the school."

In case anyone thinks their kids are better off because they live in red-state flyover country, think again!

In all my interviews and correspondence with teens, I never learned why so many keep so much hidden from their parents. Today's teens seem to have compartmentalized different aspects of their lives—school, home, church—and seem to subscribe to a "Don't ask, don't tell" policy. I mean, if you were to ask them point-blank if they ever saw fights in the hallway or gays making out at school, they might not lie about it. But they don't seem eager to volunteer specific information either.

Perhaps it comes from their desire to shield already-overburdened parents from extra stress, and the teens figure they can handle it on their own. Maybe a few are afraid their activist-type parents might rush to the school and kick up a fuss.

Or maybe it's just that when kids enter ninth grade and none of the upperclassmen seem to think it's weird to see gay people making out in the hallways, they just ignore it too.

"Desensitization" is the word the Kansas City focus group used to describe the process they've been through, comparing it to movies: just as overuse has desensitized them to bad language and homosexuality on the screen, the daily reality of teens has desensitized them to the same in-your-face defiance at school.

Yet, though they used the word "desensitization," I found the teens who talked to me to be far from desensitized. They were thoughtful, honest, vulnerable, and concerned with making it through these challenging years with their integrity intact. Some were committed to not disappoint the parents who love them. As Joanna said, "If you disappoint God, that could be the worst feeling you could ever imagine, because He's been there for you for everything. And I think it's the same with parents. Disappointing them and then looking them in the eye and seeing the hurt would be the worst feeling I could imagine."

And all were anxious to not fail—that is, to not give into temptation—knowing how much more costly the consequences would be, since any wrongdoing on their parts would damage not only their personal witness but also the reputation of Christianity.

What gives these kids the gumption to walk into school each day, knowing the challenges they have to deal with—temptations, offensive situations, attacks on their faith by peers and even teachers? What gives them the strength to live with integrity while others give in and conform?

We might say these teens must have good self-esteem—which means they must be secure in their parents' love. As Christian parents, we know it goes deeper, that they must be firmly grounded in our love and in the love of the Father.

Question: How secure are you today in God's love? In your parents' love?

Discussion Starters

Spend a rainy day organizing or looking through family photo albums with your teen or watching old family videos. If you're techno-savvy enough, teach the family how to edit and create up-to-the-minute DVDs from video footage and stills.

Along the way, talk about how your relationship is different now and how it's the same. How does your teen envision your relationship when he or she is grown?

Alyse, a homeschool student who is also very involved in the community and attends public school dances with friends: "I am completely and totally secure. I know God will love me no matter what. This doesn't mean I can do whatever I want to do—this means that if I make a mistake, God will always forgive and continue to love me. I know my parents would be there for me in a heartbeat. They love me and will always help me no matter what I do."

Rachel: "I am 100-percent sure God loves me and is working in my life. I know my parents love me for sure."

Ryan (not his real name): "I am absolutely secure in God's love. I know my parents love me because of how much they care about what I do, but sometimes it feels like they're completely angry with no love in their discipline."

Brandon: "I had an outrageous sum of God showing up *everywhere*. My relationship with Him has really matured. I can't deny that He exists and loves me without having some thought of past events flooding into my head and me shaking my head and smiling. Over the past four years or so, I've started to realized how secure I am in both God's and my parents' love, and I've been trying to figure out how to show them the same love and respect they've shown me."

Does it seem as though I've cut to the chase here? I mean, if the subject of this book is how to help teens face the crazy challenges the world is throwing at them, and barely into the first chapter it seems clear that it all boils down to making sure our kids have healthy self-esteem and are grounded in God's love, what else is there to say?

Perhaps a different writer would have arranged this book differently, building up anticipation until the climax—"All you need is love!"—was revealed. But each writer brings his or her own experience to the page, and mine is this: As a mother of 12—4 grown up and on their own, and 8 still at home—I'm still learning, too, changed by the things I discover as I research and write.

And hearing from teens who grew up in families secure in their parents' and God's love—that was a beautiful thing for someone like me who grew up without those advantages.

So let's put it right at the beginning, right where it belongs. The other principles we'll discuss to empower our kids—"Setting Limits," "Avoiding Temptation," "Developing Compassion," "Standing Up for What's Right," "Making the Most of Mistakes," and "Living with Integrity"—will be based on and infused by the spirit of God's love and our ability to demonstrate that to our kids.

 # What Does God Say?

1 Cor. 13 could stand as "The Christian Parent's Creed."

Verse 1: *If I speak in the tongues of men and of angels, but have not love, I am only a resounding gong or a clanging cymbal.*
In parenting lingo: *If I incorporate every expert parenting technique there is out there, yet fail to show my kid I care, I might as well stop talking, because it's not going to do a bit of good.*

Verses 4-5, 7: *Love is patient, love is kind . . . it is not self-seeking, it is not easily angered . . . it always protects, always trusts, always hopes, always perseveres.*
What a wonderful vision to undergird how we approach the privilege of parenting!

Make no mistake. Though I've front-loaded the foundational principle, the others are every bit as important, because they build on that foundation to produce what every loving parent—as well as our loving God—wants a child to grow into: an adult equipped to live with integrity and faith.

Love isn't just a feeling—it's a decision and a commitment: I love my child enough to do what needs to be done to help him or her reach his or her full potential. Sometimes this may not look like love on the outside. That's OK. After all, the Lord looks not at the outward appearance but at the heart (1 Sam. 16:7).

Keeping in mind that we're talking about the kind of love that has the good of the other as its goal, the simple truth remains that our number-one job as parents is to reveal God's love for our children through our own love for them—a concept so self-evident that by the time they're teens, thoughtful kids know how interconnected both loves are.

Question: As you were growing up, what did your parents do to make you feel secure in God's love and to show they loved you?

Alyse: "My parents have been awesome! Besides constantly telling me they love me and giving me hugs throughout the day, they have encouraged me in my faith with God. They check on my quiet times and will listen to me when I have questions. They have hung or posted helpful scriptures throughout the house that have helped me throughout the day. They've always been close to me and have always cared about where I am and what I'm doing. One of the best ways parents can show their kids they care is to tell them and to ask about how their lives are going. Even though sometimes teenagers feel their parents are just butting in, it helps a lot and encourages them to do the right thing."

Kristen: "My parents took me to church and were always interested in what I had going on, and they encouraged me to do my best. They came to my sports games and art shows. It meant a lot to me. They also prayed with me when I was little."

Brandon: "My parents showed it through their actions and their words. I don't believe I really took to heart what they were saying until I was about 13 years old. That's when I really started to think about what God's love, my parents' love, and love in general meant and what it means to love them in return."

Joshua: "My parents showed me God's love by letting me make mistakes and then talking about them afterwards. They also showed it through discipline."

Sarah: "My parents always prayed with me if I was going through a hard time. They were always available if I wanted to talk about something. When I had a problem at school that needed to be addressed, they followed through. If I'm sick or depressed, my mother always stays home with me. They make time for me even if they're in the middle of doing something. If I need help on my homework, my Dad always stops what he's doing to take a look."

Rick: "My mom and dad always tell me they love me and how much they love me, and that makes so much of a difference. And my parents tell me that God loves me even more than they can, and they show how much they love me every day. They take care of me when I'm sick, and they buy me stuff. We wouldn't be able to survive without our parents. And I know my parents will love me no matter what, and if God loves me even more than that, that's awesome."

Rick's response illustrates perfectly how the parent-child relationship influences—for better or worse—the teens' later image of and relationship with God. This is a great responsibility for parents. A mother or father who is aloof, uninvolved, or uncaring can cripple a child's ability to comprehend and receive the Heavenly Father's love (although, as I can attest, His love can overcome any emotional handicap). Kids whose parents are committed and caring will find it most natural to feel assured of God's love and to trust Him.

In addition, to realize the full potential of the parent-child relationship—and the full potential of your child's relationship to God—your child must respect you and must be willing to submit to your authority. A child who doesn't respect and submit to his or her parents finds it much more difficult to respect and submit to God.

Get Involved!

A Simple Recipe for Success

Want to maximize your children's chances for success? Want to boost their grades and SAT scores, develop good self-esteem and social skills—plus help them avoid cigarettes, drugs, and alcohol?

Show them you care in just 30 minutes a day. Eat dinner with them.

If your house is more "Little House on the Freeway" than "Little House on the Prairie," here's how:

Keep dinnertime flexible. On nights Zach has karate, we have dinner at 5:00. On nights Ben has rehearsal, we have it at 7:00. I look for a window of opportunity—and if we can't all be home, then at least when most of us will be.

Use a crock pot. First thing in the morning, throw in some meat, mushroom soup, and onion soup mix—or try spaghetti sauce with defrosted frozen meatballs.

Cut back on computer time to make room for a meal together. During dinner, turn off the television set, and don't answer the phone.

Keep things simple. Once a week we do "breakfast night"—pancakes, sausage, eggs.

No matter how simple the meal, candles make it special.

The bottom line is this: Kids don't care if it's fish sticks and french fries as long as time with you is on the menu.

Self-esteem is tied to knowing God's love for us. As parents, we have an obligation to do everything we can to bring our children to that level of self esteem.

In the transition from sweet little just-adores-Mommy-and-Daddy child to awkward, porcupine-quill-like teen years, some things will change. Sometimes the reorientation in the parent-child relationship resembles the shift of tectonic plates, complete with earthquakes and aftershocks.

Some parents buckle at the first tremors and never regain

Discussion Starters

Teenagers love to talk. But it's not enough to ask, "How was your day?"

When psychologist Torey Hayden asked several hundred teens what they wished they could talk with their parents about, they named—

- Family matters—vacations, decisions, rules, curfews, serious illness, money problems.
- Controversial issues—sex, lifestyles, drugs.
- Emotional issues—parents' feelings about them and other things.
- Big whys—why people go hungry, why there is war, and other philosophical issues.
- The future—work, college, making plans for life beyond life in the current home.
- Current affairs—world and community happenings.
- Personal interest—sports, hobbies, friends.
- Parents themselves—what parents were like when they were young, stories that show parents are real.

Adapted from *ERIC Digest,* "Parenting Teens" by Karen DeBord, Ph.D., State Extension Specialist, Child Development North Carolina Cooperative Extension.

control. Some seem to think that by the 13th or 14th birthday, they've taught their kids everything they need to know about family and relationships, and now it's up to the kids to make their own decisions about friends, dating, partying, and curfews.

Families I've met with this philosophy—and they really do exist—no matter how religious, generally produce kids who are out of control.

The area where I live has certainly seen its share of the effects of out-of-control teens. In the last four months, 17 teens in the Washington metro area have died in car crashes, provoking a huge outcry to raise the driving age from 16 to 17 or 18. But when you read closely, you discover the accidents involve 16-

year-olds driving home drunk from parties, guys driving home from strip clubs at four in the morning, deciding to see how fast their cars would go.

The big question: where were their parents? And the next big question: is it fair to take away driving privileges from the thousands of responsible, law-abiding 16-year-olds? How about all those teens who have after-school jobs or help their parents shuttle younger siblings around? If you really think about it, wouldn't you guess that responsible teens far outnumber those whose parents have not enforced curfews or boundaries?

We'll be discussing the need for parental oversight more in "Setting Limits," but I bring it up now to make the point that for parents, loving your children must involve continuing to be involved in their lives, particularly where safety is concerned.

At a school board meeting last year, I saw a father come forward with this tale of woe: His daughter had been driving friends home from a party when she was pulled over and charged with driving under the influence (DUI). In addition to her legal woes, a DUI in Loudoun County, Virginia, means a student is pulled from any athletic team. The father was pleading for an exception for his daughter, arguing and rationalizing that with two working parents and no after-school supervision at home, now more than ever she needed her team to strengthen her character.

Actually, as football coach John Wooden once said, "Sports do not build character . . . they reveal it." This daughter had already demonstrated that being involved in athletics was not enough to keep her on the straight and narrow. Now it was a lesson she—and her dad—would have another chance to learn, but in a harder way.

The pleading father wasn't thinking long-term about the woman his daughter will grow to become. Otherwise, rather than pleading with the school board, he would be reinforcing the lessons she needed to learn. What about those friends who might have been killed? He might explain to her why she needed to experience the consequences of her decisions and how she would become a better person if she accepted them in the right spirit.

As a parent, I know how hard it is to see your child go through consequences that hurt. And I've certainly been guilty on occasion of being merciful when mercy wasn't warranted. But I've learned that it only delays the lesson my child needs to learn and that God will undoubtedly supply another opportunity for him or her to learn it. Might as well get it over now instead of later.

 # Get Involved!

Rethinking Living Spaces to Encourage Family Togetherness

You can capture more top-quality moments by increasing unstructured quantity time. But for parents with other demands on their time, how?

- Reorient your home so that bedrooms are for sleeping and changing clothes.
- Move desks, computers, and television sets out of the bedrooms.
- Reorganize your family room to accommodate all computers, study places.
- Have only one television set the whole family watches together, or just one extra for younger siblings.
- Make the kitchen inviting, and encourage kids to help with cooking, sharing about your days.

Love means involvement in your children's lives before they get into trouble. With four teenage sons, I meet more than my share of teenagers, and there are some who you just know are headed in the wrong direction. Some come from divorced families and so are at risk. Having their parents divorce is just about the worst thing that can happen to children.

Remember when couples in conflict stayed together for the sake of the children? Now it has become fashionable for parents to do what's right for themselves, rationalizing that it was better for the kids to be free of the parents' conflict.

That was never true.

Today's research shows that children do better in two-parent families even if the parents are at odds (the exception being if there is violence in the home). So perhaps the most loving thing parents can do for their children is to honor their own wedding vows—for better, for worse, for richer, for poorer, in sickness, and in health, until death.

Statistics show that children from fatherless homes are five times more likely to commit suicide, 32 times more likely to run away, 20 times more likely to end up in prison, and 73 percent more likely to be fatally abused.

But statistics aside, there's a difference in everyday behavior. I have particular compassion for girls growing up without involved dads. Having grown up fatherless myself, I understand the hole in the souls of fatherless girls. My prayer for each fatherless girl I know is that she'll come to know God's love in such a powerful way that she won't feel incomplete without a guy in her life.

When a 14-year-old girl my children go to church with got pregnant, it led to a big family discussion about her out-of-control behavior, her relationship with her father, and the way her pregnancy was being handled. Was a big family discussion about someone else's problems appropriate? I emphatically believe it was.

Sometimes Christians stifle discussion by labeling it gossip, consequently losing the opportunity to process events and learn from the mistakes of others. It's one thing to make a list of what makes a good father and another to receive instruction from a true-life story. Isn't that what the Bible, a collection of stories about people who often made mistakes, is all about? I believe my sons will be better fathers for it. I wanted my boys to see the importance of fathers watching out for their daughters' purity.

While girls without an involved father figure sometimes seem to have a heightened need for male attention, the ones whose still-married parents have set no boundaries may have difficulty knowing how to handle their freedom. When the teenager is too young to wisely handle these freedoms, she can be easily led down the path of promiscuity or to self-loathing, which sometimes manifests in food disorders or self-injurious behavior like cutting. The path of immorality often leads to feelings of low self-worth and hopelessness.

As tough as the absence of a father is on a girl, living with a dad who doesn't care enough to protect his daughter is worse. An abandoned daughter may cling to the hope that though her father left, way down deep he really cared for her. For the unprotected daughter, her father's lack of concern for her welfare strips away any hope that she's worthy of love.

Think of it this way: self-esteem, so closely tied with the comprehension of the sanctity of life, is based on relationship with the Heavenly Father and the experience of His love. In the same way, the love of her earthly father plays a key role in the formation of a young woman's self-concept.

Sometimes daddies grow uneasy as their little girls mature into young women. When your daughter tries to snuggle close the way she did when she was a little girl, the best thing is to think of her as your little girl and hold her just the way you did when you were a beginning daddy. There's a part of every woman that still longs to be Daddy's little girl, to feel completely safe and protected. Though my own earthly father isn't there for me, I feel that way about my Heavenly Father, as though I'll always—even when I'm gray—be his little girl.

When my second daughter, Jasmine, was 13, Tripp took her on a date. Tripp is actually Jasmine's stepfather—we married when Samantha was 13 and Jasmine was 7—but he raised both girls as his own. And even though they have a strong relationship with their birth father, since Tripp and I and the girls became Christians in 1987, he is more their spiritual father.

It was as her spiritual father that Tripp was inspired to take her on her first date. He asked her in advance, cleaned the car, dressed up, brought her flowers, and took her to dinner. All the while he played the perfect gentleman—opening her door, taking her coat, pulling out her chair, asking what she would like and then ordering for her. While Jasmine would not be dating for several years, Tripp wanted to plant the idea that she was a wonderful treasure and should expect any guy who asked her out to treat her with a lot of consideration and respect.

Sixteen years later, as our family sat around the Thanksgiving table sharing things we were thankful for, Jasmine recounted that date with her dad as life-changing, because it set her expectations high, and she never gave her heart away until someone capable of such devotion appeared in her life.

She was 23 when she met Nathan, and today they're married with four children.

Jasmine also thanked Tripp for praying every night for her future mate. It gave her a sense that her life was important, that it had meaning beyond her next play, her next report card, her next party. To be reminded daily that God had a plan for her life, a plan that involved someone He already knew would

What Does God Say?

Our society tends to look at children as financial burdens, as in "We would like to have had more, but we couldn't afford them." Not so in the ancient Hebrew culture, as in many cultures today, where children are regarded as unqualified blessings, representing our stake in the future:

Sons are a heritage from the LORD, children a reward from him. Like arrows in the hands of a warrior are sons born in one's youth. Blessed is the man whose quiver is full of them. They will not be put to shame when they contend with their enemies in the gate (Ps. 127:3-5).

someday be her husband—that made her feel very, very special and very loved.

Boys need attention, too, and guidance when it comes to friendships, dating, and how they spend their time. One of the best pieces of advice I ever received about raising boys came from a mother of six boys I knew many years ago and who is now Samantha's mother-in-law. She said, "Make sure they get jobs in restaurants. That will keep them too busy to get into trouble and will give them plenty to eat." She wasn't kidding.

If girls need to feel protected, my experience is that boys need to feel useful. I know that a couple of mine can seem like lazy lugs sometimes—only interested in sleeping late and playing video games—but when they're working at something that makes them feel necessary and/or irreplaceable, they really shine. Sometimes it may feel as if you're pulling a mule up a steep slope to get your son to start a project, but once it's started, there's a male momentum that keeps him on track, especially if you're lavishing him with praise.

"Lavish" is a good word also when it comes to considering how to love your teens. As they grow into adulthood, we tend sometimes to think they're more self-sufficient than they truly are. But the fact is, they need us as much as ever, just in a different way.

Teens still need to respect their parents and obey them. And we still need to be fully available to our teens. Your relationship may look different than it looked when you were there to pick them up after a fall, to kiss their injuries and make them better. Your relationship may look different, but there will be times your teens will need your tender words of comfort when they take an emotional spill.

Jesus said, "Whoever welcomes one of these little children in my name welcomes me; and whoever welcomes me does not welcome me but the one who sent me" (Mark 9:37). When I remember this, I want to love my teen lavishly.

Loving them lavishly can be as simple as stopping what

you're doing when they want to talk. Make good eye contact. Be an active listener with vocal and facial responses that encourage them to continue talking. And don't forget tactile activities—holding hands and hugging.

Loving them lavishly can mean sitting down with them to watch their favorite television show or movie and asking why they like it. It might mean turning off the radio in the car and starting conversations about special memories you've shared or questions they can't resist—questions focused on them.

When they were little, you used to create photo ops to capture memories. Loving them lavishly now means creating conversation ops—going for walks, gardening, painting a room, or doing a jigsaw puzzle together.

Loving them lavishly means continuing to do favorite family activities together and maybe exploring some new territory. If your family is into camping and hiking, try visiting a dinner theater or museum—and vice-versa.

Loving them lavishly means continuing to pray with them before they go to bed, leaving Post-it notes with special Bible verses on the bathroom mirror or steering wheel, encouraging them to come to you with their problems, maintaining your cool, and forgiving them when they've done wrong—and always reminding them with three simple words: "I love you."

Bottom Line for Parents

- Model God's love.
- Allow consequences.
- Protect daughters.
- Help sons feel useful.
- Encourage conversation.
- Love lavishly.

2. SETTING LIMITS

Self-assurance

"When can I start dating?" Madeleine asked me shortly after starting middle school.

My goodness! I thought. *She's only 11!* But once we had talked a little, I could see where the pressure was coming from.

First of all, some of her friends had started going out with guys at school. As kids have explained it to me, "going out" isn't actually dating. It just means a boy and a girl like each other and often through the use of proxies—as in "Jenny, will you find out if Gabe wants to go out with me?"—officially become a couple. This means they walk to class together, with or without hand-holding, and talk on the phone after school.

But beyond that, some of Maddy's sixth-grade friends had actually started dating—being driven as a couple to the movies or bowling by one of the moms.

It was as though the kids had left the predictable culture of elementary school and, upon entering the doors of middle school, entered a new territory filled with possibilities.

But this wasn't new territory for me since Maddy is my ninth child. I've been through it all before.

It took me back to the days when my first daughter, Samantha, now (gasp!) 35, went on her first date with a boy named Max. He appeared at our door freshly groomed and walked her out to the car where his mom waited. When Samantha came home, she had a new necklace he had given her as a Christmas present.

I thought it was all very cute. I couldn't understand why Samantha didn't want to go out with him again.

Perhaps she had more common sense than I.

I confess. I was once a permissive parent. Having grown up with no spiritual foundation or moral guidelines myself, I didn't have anything really to pass on. And since my background wasn't undergirded with love, I had no understanding of what parental love looked like.

During the 1970s and early 1980s, as a member of the counterculture, I counted personal freedom as top priority. I ended up thinking that by giving my children a lot of freedom, I was demonstrating my love.

My kids didn't even have set bedtimes.

All that began to change when Samantha was a high school junior. She had begun dating a boy she had known since we moved to Marin County, California, from San Francisco when she was in fifth grade. He remembers her ethnic city style, which stood out in a more preppy culture. We remember his showing up for their first date in white pants and a turquoise shirt and Samantha coming down the stairs in white pants and turquoise shirt (this was the 1980s). As a friend put it, "They look like figures on a wedding cake." Later they were.

But in the meantime, we all had a lot of growing-up to do.

Typical of my parenting style, I never told Samantha what time I expected her to come home. But when at some point in her junior year she started coming in from dates with Kip at two in the morning, I had to confront the obvious: kids just don't always make good choices.

Tripp and I gave Sam a curfew. Later, passing by her bedroom, I heard her on the phone bragging to a friend, "My parents gave me a curfew. I have to be home by 12 from now on."

The funny thing was, she sounded quite happy. She was proud, even, that her parents were doing their job.

I began to realize that my permissive parenting style—

which I would have confidently told you demonstrated my love and trust—was sending the opposite message: "I don't care."

I began to see that kids need limits even during their teens.

Kids don't just need limits—they secretly want them. Fortunately I discovered this in time to ditch the permissive parenting and do a better job raising Samantha's younger brothers and sisters. Kids need to know someone's in charge—that parents care enough to think through what's best for them and then stand by their standards no matter how uncomfortable things get.

Consider this: Researchers have observed that groups of schoolchildren on an unfenced playground tend to huddle together—too timid to venture very far. When the playground is fenced, the children—feeling more secure—spread far and wide, making every bit of space their own.

Limits are like the guardrails that keep us from plunging off a bridge. They're there to protect us—an instrument not of oppression but of love. By making clear boundaries, parents demonstrate their love while empowering their children to explore life with an assurance of well-being and safety.

But let's hear what kids themselves have to say.

Question: Do your parents set boundaries? How do you feel about them?

Alyse: "Of course my parents set boundaries. As I grew up, my boundaries changed from 'Don't use the stove' to 'Don't do drugs.' Sometimes I don't agree with the new rules, but I learn very quickly why they made them. I have to let my parents know exactly what's going to happen when I'm out for the evening with my friends. At first I didn't understand this rule, because teenagers don't tend to be good planners. Now I've learned that this rule keeps my friends and me from just hanging out in parking lots trying to decide what to do. We get together, go out, have fun, then come home.

Joel: "My parents set some boundaries. Sometimes it seems they go beyond just trying to protect me, but then sometimes I see later that they've helped me in my growth with God."

Kristen: "My parents were a little overprotective, I think, but I'm glad now that they were. If I had gotten into the habits some of my friends got in, I would not be as responsible academically and spiritually as I am now."

These kids sound accepting of the limits their parents have set, but my guess is that their answers might take their parents by surprise. Often, with time for reflection, even teens can see the good in something that had them kicking and screaming earlier.

Kids are kids, and even if they know and understand that they need limits, they're probably not about to let their parents know that. Their job is to keep pushing and testing their limits. Our job is to stay focused on what's best for them.

One thing I learned from the Kansas City focus group was this: parents can make their own jobs easier if they enable their kids to understand the reasons behind the boundaries they set. Matt put it this way: "I think what's important is for parents to explain why instead of setting those boundaries and that being that. That will just lead to rebellion."

And Michael, whose answers consistently indicated a loving, trusting relationship with his parents, said, "If they communicate it to you as love instead of 'This is how it's going to be,' then it makes a big difference. Because I know my parents love me and that's why they care. If I thought they were just doing it to make my life miserable, then I might look at it a little differently. But parents can communicate to their kids that the reason they care so much is because they want you to do well and they don't want you to make bad decisions, instead of just 'I'm doing this because I'm the parent, and that's what I'm supposed to do.'"

Actually, letting our kids know why we set the limits we do is helpful in more ways than one. Since one aspect of our job as parents is to equip our children to become good parents themselves—making wise decisions on behalf of our *grandchildren*—taking the time to explain how we arrive at our decisions is an integral part of their training and instruction as future parents.

What Does God Say?

Fathers, do not embitter your children,
or they will become discouraged (Col. 3:21).

Fathers, do not exasperate your children; Instead, bring them
up in the training and instruction of the Lord (Eph. 6:4).

Again and again, I heard from teens the importance of knowing that the limits their parents set had been thought out and were not just off the top of their heads or arbitrary. If, for example, I answered Maddy's question by saying she could date at 16, it sounds as though I've just pulled a number out of a hat. There's not much credibility there.

Since I wanted the limit to have meaning for her, to give her a better chance to embrace it herself, I took my time, asked her some questions, talked things through.

As we talked, it became apparent to me that Maddy actually wasn't interested in dating right now herself, but the fact that some other girls were dating made her curious in a theoretical sort of way. But she could see the dating issue had ramifications beyond simply going somewhere with a guy. She had noticed that her friends who were dating, or even "going out," had less time for girlfriend fun. The girls who were dating early tended to wear makeup early and sometimes seemed to push the limits of the school dress code.

It was a wonderful opportunity for me to tell Madeleine how wise it is not to be in a hurry to grow up and how important the next few years would be for her in setting a good academic foundation for high school. We talked about how much more fun she would have focusing on friendships with girls and boys rather than complicating her life too soon with a boyfriend.

Discussion Starters

- Why are some girls eager to date?
- Why do some parents have different rules about dating?
- What's happening with your friends who've started dating? Have they changed?
- What are some reasons it might be better to wait to date?

It was also an opportunity to remind her of the most important reason her dad and I set limits: we love her and want to protect her.

The fact is that girls who date early are more at risk. That's the message of a 27-page report published by the National Campaign to Prevent Teen Pregnancy that incorporates research from Yale, Columbia, and the University of California. It's called *14 and Younger: The Sexual Behavior of Young Adolescents*, and you can download a copy at <http://www.teen pregnancy.org/resources/reading/pdf/14summary.pdf>.

Among the conclusions: Approximately one in five kids has sex by age 15. Early dating leads to early sex. Early first sexual experiences for girls are more likely to be unwanted. Girls dating older boys are very vulnerable to early and unwanted sex. Sexually experienced kids under 15 are more likely to use drugs and alcohol. And girls who have sex before age 15 are more likely to become promiscuous or pregnant, contract a sexually transmitted disease, or drop out of high school.

While I didn't burden Madeleine with all the details—she's only 11, after all—I gave her enough information to let her know that waiting to date was something she would be glad she did later on. Since I didn't want her to come off as judgmental with her dating friends, I also explained what I've so often explained to all my kids: different families have different standards. As believers, we'll find our standards are bound to set us apart in some ways. We can't just blindly follow what others do. We have to ask questions, look for God's best in our lives, and trust that He will guide our family's decision making. The best thing Madeleine can do for unbelieving friends is to be loving and kind, pray for them, and be ready to share what a difference Jesus has made in her life.

It's important for our children to have this larger view of us as parents, to know we're not just reveling in our authority over them but that we're the instruments God has provided to keep them on track. If they understand we're trying to meet the responsibility God has given us and leaning on Him for guidance, they're better equipped to trust us.

There are some things just out and out wrong because they are forbidden by commandments—like cheating or shoplifting.

There are things that are illegal—like underage drinking, drugs, speeding.

Some kids would never dream of breaking these rules. But what happens when something unexpected happens, something for which they're not prepared?

Like some diseases, sin can strike suddenly. Because we can't bring our kids up in a protective bubble like someone with a rare autoimmune disorder, they'll encounter risky moments like arriving at an out-of-control party or accidentally stumbling onto a porn site or answering the door after school while parents are at work and seeing the guy you've had a crush on standing there with his books "to do a little homework together."

Many of the teens I interviewed who had made a bad choice —that is, done something they knew was wrong and/or something their parents wouldn't approve of—reported feeling dazed and confused when faced suddenly and unexpectedly with a new situation. Under pressure, they tended to go with the flow.

One idea from our Kansas City focus group was for parents to help their kids anticipate potential problems and discuss strategies—as we do when our kids are learning to drive and we teach them it's not enough to drive well but to drive defensively. We say things like "What would you do if that car across from us tried to beat you on the green light and took a fast left?" We try to prepare them for every eventuality.

We can do that with their daily teenage lives too. We can prepare them for the inevitable bumps in the road—the sticky situations and risky moments that can sneak up and surprise them—by anticipating them in advance, equipping them with strategies to keep them safe, and building their confidence as they practice saying no.

In addition, your teens need to know you're always there for them. Give them a cell phone and let them know you're just a

Get Involved!

Protect your children through role playing. Here are a few ideas to get you started:

- You're shopping with your friend. She takes a bottle of nail polish off the shelf and puts it into her jacket pocket. What do you do?
- Your teacher has the class grading each other's papers. The kid next to you wants to change his incorrect answer before you mark it. What happens next?
- You're at the movies with a bunch of friends when a guy you've seen around school comes over and offers a bunch of little smiley-face paper squares. "Eat one of these. You'll like the movie," he says. Before anyone can say anything else, a couple of your friends go for it. What about you?
- You're invited to a party, but you get there and find out the parents aren't home. You start to leave, but your friends tease you. What do you do?
- You're at the football game and a friend hands you a bottle of Coke. You start to take a drink and then realize it smells like alcohol. What do you do?

phone call away, that you'll come get them out of any difficult situation at any time.

Michael, one of our Kansas City focus group, shared this strategy: "My parents have always told me if there's something I don't think is right or I don't want to do, but I don't want to be the one to say anything, they're like 'Just blame it on us— we'll be the bad guys.'"

When teens understand that the reason you set limits is to protect them, they're much more inclined to accept the limits you set. Since their protection is most likely the reason behind any limits you set, the key is to take the time to express that.

That doesn't mean that kids won't balk or even get angry. Still, the bottom line is that parents are in charge and need to stick with limits—unless new information calls for reconsideration—no matter what their teens say.

My visit to Kansas City coincided with the September 13, 2004, edition of *Newsweek*, which featured a cover story called "The Power of No," about the difficulties that parents today seem to be having in saying no to their kids.

When asked about their reaction to the story, the focus group was adamant that parents should say no.

Joanna: "They should say no. . . . I don't like it very much, but in the long run, you think back to it, and you're like 'Yeah, I shouldn't have done that anyway.'"

Rick: "When parents say no, they're not doing it to be mean, but they're doing it because they know what's best for us. Like my dad, there's nothing I can do that he doesn't know about, because he's done it all before. He was a teenage guy, so if he says no, that I shouldn't do it, that it's probably not good for me, he's not doing it to be mean or a jerk or anything."

Can parents be jerks about setting limits? Yes, I believe we can—any time we set limits in an arbitrary fashion, without good reason, or as a knee-jerk reaction.

Here's an example: When my son Ben was 13, he decided

that more than anything he wanted one of his ears pierced. It was 1996, and we were living in California, so it wasn't completely unusual for a middle school guy to have a pierced ear. However, at that time in the Christian community—even in California—it was extremely rare to see a guy with an earring.

My husband, Tripp, automatically said no. Ben was crushed. He seemed to have a lot of his "identity" tied up in this. He had been growing his hair a little longer and dressing a little more "bohemian," so I figured he was trying to establish a more interesting image. I thought a pierced ear would be OK.

Here's how I explained my reasoning to Tripp: "We say no to sex, no to drugs, no to alcohol. If we say no to a pierced ear, this just gives it the same status as the other forbidden things. I think if we say yes whenever possible, it will make saying no more meaningful."

After prayer and thought, Tripp had a change of heart and agreed. He told Ben that he could indeed get one ear pierced. The lesson for us: be open to God's wisdom and discernment, to rethinking a situation, and to possibly telling your child, "We've thought this over and changed our minds."

If you know Ben today, you're probably wondering where this is going, since Ben does not have a pierced ear. Oh, but he did for a while. After his dad told him we had reconsidered and why, Ben wasted no time getting down to the mall and having a teeny gold ball shot into his lobe.

Our friends—believers and nonbelievers—were shocked. *The Curtises? They did what? Are you sure?* Keep in mind this was almost 10 years ago. It required a lot of outside-the-box thinking for people to wrap their minds around the fact that a loving-but-somewhat-on-the-strict-side family had allowed a son to get an ear pierced.

When I explained our reasoning, I could see the light go on for some of my friends, while others nodded their heads doubtfully, still in the dark about how and why we could allow such nonconformity.

But pierced ears were not an issue for very long. It was only a matter of a couple weeks before Ben lost interest and took his earring out.

All I could think was how horrible it would have been if we had forbidden the earring and perhaps planted seeds of rebellion in our son. The earring incident helped Tripp and me see how important it is not to go with our own Christian cultural flow but to truly zero in on individual situations, seeking God's wisdom and then implementing it to the best of our ability.

To this day, I'm grateful God gave us the opportunity to say yes to something we might not have preferred but which didn't really put Ben in harm's way so that the truly harmful things would remain in a class by themselves and there would be no confusion caused by ear piercing being lumped in the same forbidden territory as alcohol, drugs, or sex—all of which Ben has managed to stay clear of to this day.

As far as the nonnegotiables go, it's wise to take a proactive approach. That means not leaving it up to public school to educate your teens about sex, for instance, because the school's worldview has been stripped of God. And as believers, our understanding of sex, as well as everything else, should be based on our understanding of God and His plan for our lives.

When it comes to the sex education—sometimes called "family life"—offered in public schools, you may or may not decide to exercise your parental right to opt your kids out of these classes. I highly recommend reviewing the materials that will be used in class, and if you feel comfortable enough to leave your child in the class, augment the secular approach by sharing the biblical approach with your children yourself. Otherwise, our kids' idea of sex can be compartmentalized and separated from the concept of marriage and family.

Having grown up as children of divorce in non-Christian homes, as new believers, and by then parents of five, Tripp and I thought carefully about how God might want us to approach the issue of marriage and sex with our kids. We knew it was im-

Discussion Starters

For Mom and Dad to decide together
What are our nonnegotiables?
   Must-nots: drugs, alcohol, sex, pornography.
   Musts: seatbelts, modest clothing, chores.
What is negotiable?
   Bedtimes, some piercings and tattoos, hair color, food choices.

In thinking through individual situations, choose your battles wisely. Be guided by WWJD? rather than by WWPT? That is, *What would Jesus do?* rather than *What would people think?*

portant for them to hear it from us first. So we started early with a simple plan.

The concept of purity isn't a turning-away from sex but a turning *toward* God. It isn't like Just Say No to Drugs. Drugs are bad for you, so we say no. Sex is good, so we don't say no—we say *wait*. Wait until your wedding night.

We also go over the practical benefits of purity: studies show that married couples enjoy sex the most and that those who have only one partner and who wait for marriage report the highest satisfaction of all. This just goes to show that following God's plan really does produce the best outcome!

When our children turn 13, Tripp takes the birthday boy camping, or I take the birthday girl to a fancy hotel, where we do some more talking about these matters and ask for a commitment to remain pure and to preserve the special gift God has given them for their future husband or wife. Six of our children so far have made that commitment. (One broke it, but I talk about how that happened and how we handled it in the chapter titled "Making the Most of Mistakes.") Some of our kids have decided to wear a promise ring as a reminder.

Get Involved!

*In today's world—where sex is cheap and easy to come by—
we can help our kids by giving them a vision of what sex is really
all about and how valuable it is. Here's what Tripp and I try to
pass on to ours:*

Just as every car has an owner's manual to help us understand and keep it at its best, the Bible is God's owner's manual
for His creation. Things go best for us when we follow what God
says.

God's plan is one husband, one wife—no sex outside this
sacred union.

It's not really so much about sex being forbidden but about
its being reserved so that it can fulfill His plan for marriage.
That's because sex is such an incredibly wonderful experience
that when a husband and wife have their first sex together,
they're bound together more securely.

It's the exquisite richness of this experience that makes it
worth waiting for. So as you grow up, even though your body
may send signals that it's ready for sex and even though you
may want it, you wait in order to make that moment in your
marriage as special as it was meant to be.

God can help you.

Coming home doesn't mean the end of the discussion by
any means. I'm pleased that my children don't treat sex as a
taboo subject but as something we can talk about and even kid
around about—as when my boys somehow think they'll have
great sexual prowess because their own father had a lot of kids.

I use sex as the example here, but the same principles apply
to setting limits for anything—drugs, alcohol, music, movies,
dating, and curfew. The important thing is to talk about your
expectations *beforehand*, so that when your child reaches the
age when it becomes an issue, you've already built a foundation.

When you suspect your child is ignoring the limits you

set—drinking at parties, for example—confront your child and hold him or her accountable, all the while reassuring him or her of your love. Our teens need us not just to establish limits, but they also need to know we care enough to enforce them.

Every parent needs a vision, a plan, and clearly communicated limits. I didn't have these 25 years ago, when Samantha was growing up. I hadn't been brought up with a firm foundation myself. Not yet a believer, I didn't understand my responsibilities as a parent.

Nowadays I find there are a lot of parents like the one I once was, parents who think the laissez-faire—"kids will be kids"—approach to parenting will work. Sometimes even parents who

What Does God Say?

A Spoonful of Scripture

Mary Poppins sang, "Just a spoonful of sugar helps the medicine go down," as she charmed her charges into doing their chores. Likewise, a spoonful of scripture will help our teens understand and appreciate the limits we set.

Children, obey your parents in the Lord, for this is right.

"Honor your father and mother—which is the first commandment with a promise—"that it may go well with you and that you may enjoy long life on the earth" (Eph. 6:1-3).

My son, do not forget my teaching, but keep my commands in your heart, for they will prolong your life many years and bring you prosperity (Prov. 3:1-2).

Listen to advice and accept instruction, and in the end you will be wise (Prov. 19:20).

did set limits when their children were younger think that somehow they should back off when their children are teens.

On October 12, 2004, *USA Today* covered a study by Synovate, a research market firm. This study found that 43 percent of parents wanted to be their child's best friend. "Some parents feel their own parents didn't understand them, and they see a best friend as someone who is fun to be around, listens, and is nonjudgmental." But unlike a traditional parent, a best-friend parent "doesn't give you rules and tell you what to do," according to Ian Pierpont, Synovate senior vice president. "One mother wouldn't make her child do homework because it would make him unhappy," Pierpont says. "The majority of best-friend parents are just not setting guidelines and rules" (Nancy Helmich, "Parents Want to Be Teens' Pals," *USA Today*, October 12, 2004. <http://www.usatoday.com/news/health/2004-10-12-parents-usat_x.htm>.

That explains a lot—like the times I call to check on my teen's whereabouts or to find out why he or she is late for curfew and the parent on the other end acts as if I'm a weirdo. Or why when I call to introduce myself to the parents of someone one of my kids is going out with—so maybe we can see if we're on the same page when it comes to dating guidelines—they sound defensive.

What is driving this new parenting trend? Some experts think one factor is that with both parents working outside the home, parents are so highly motivated to enjoy their family time that they avoid anything that might create tension or conflict.

Like best-friend parents, I want to be loving and understanding. I would like to avoid tension and conflict. But I also know I have a job to do in terms of guiding my kids through these important years.

What's ironic is that many parents are moving away from setting limits just as kids are more in need of them.

Consider: When Samantha was growing up in the 1980s, our society in general pretty much agreed on what was right and what was wrong. Those kids weren't bombarded from their toddler years with sexual imagery and music. Parents, trying to bring up responsible young adults, weren't clashing with hedonistic worldviews that granted kids a lot of license.

Though my child was ultimately my responsibility, I also had a lot of support from the culture. Certain behaviors, like sex before marriage, were wrong, plain and simple. Sure, kids made mistakes, but when they did there were consequences and shame to deal with. Consequently, there weren't that many mistakes.

But three decades later, that's all changed. Today's television shows and music and movies portray sex as easygoing fun and barely worth a second thought. Ads for herpes medications make it clear that even a sexually transmitted disease doesn't have to get in the way of having sex whenever you want. They've had the same impact on kids that seeing their favorite stars smoking does—which is why there are groups completely devoted to getting smoking out of movies.

The result? While in the 1960s the average age of first intercourse for women was around 18, today it's 16, even as the average age for marriage has increased. That means, for parents who are serious about helping their kids maintain their purity, setting clearly defined boundaries is more necessary and important than ever.

Even as the increasing need for clear boundaries is clashing with the trend for parents to be pals, Tripp and I have stood our ground—continuing to set limits we think appropriate, even when our kids balk, even when other parents act as if we're from another planet.

In today's culture it can be difficult to be a traditional parent when other parents are way more "cool"—dressing like their kids, hanging out with them, and being laid back. However, as much as parents might like it, the kids themselves are not so thrilled. Only 28 per cent of teens and young adults say they intend to be a best friend to their own children.

And here are comments made in the Kansas City focus group:

"Parents should not try to live through their kids. This is not a good thing for either of them."

"What teens really want is a parent, not a friend. We have lots of friends."

"I want my mom to be my mom."

I found these comments very reassuring! As a mom, I get the same sort of feedback from my children as any parent. But as a writer, I was privileged to see some things in the hearts of teenagers I might never have seen in my own—things these kids' moms perhaps have never seen either.

Though I've already brought five kids through high school —and six through driver's training—I've learned a little more from my experience preparing to write this book. Having heard from other teenagers, I'm a better parent for my own.

It's never too late to learn.

Bottom Line for Parents

- Set limits.
- Explain your reasons.
- Choose your battles wisely.
- Empower your kids to say no.
- Be a parent, not a pal.

3. AVOIDING TEMPTATION

Self-control

I remember a classmate named Peggy at the Catholic high school I attended. By far the cutest and peppiest cheerleader, she had everything the rest of us girls wanted—including a boyfriend on the football team. I was nerd enough to feel special when Peggy nudged me during history class to slide my paper a little left so she could copy my answers. That was about as close to the popular crowd as I ever got.

In our senior year, Peggy suddenly disappeared with no warning or explanation. You could almost feel the hush around her empty desk. After a time, the whispers began—whispers that the most popular girl in our class was pregnant, that her parents had shipped her off somewhere to have the baby. We never saw her again.

It was the 1960s, and we were so innocent. My friends and I couldn't begin to grasp the idea of someone our age having a baby. We couldn't even begin to grasp the idea that Peggy had sex. Was it possible that maybe she had gotten pregnant just from making out?

Those were the days! And while I'm not suggesting that they were perfect or that the problem of teenage pregnancy didn't exist, I'm invoking the past for a moment to make a point—and the point is this:

Parents today have to work much harder to help their kids avoid making mistakes than parents of previous generations.

The momentum began in the late 1960s with the sexual revolution, the free love movement, and radical feminism—all based on the notion that women and men have the same sexual nature and that any limits placed on sexual expression by society or religion are wrong.

What began as a fringe idea—far removed from the traditional values of mainstream America—went on over the next 40 years to become mainstream so that by 2002 more than one third of babies born in the United States were born to unwed mothers—from high school girls like Peggy to grown-up women on their own or in a living-together situation.

Big factors in the promotion of female sexual liberty and the acceptance of unmarried motherhood include the introduction of "the pill" in the '60s, the legalization of abortion in

 Get Involved!

Even if you're teaching your teens to remain abstinent before marriage, you need to know what the world wants to teach your kids about sex. Public school teens committed to abstinence are under a lot of pressure, surrounded by peers who have been taught they have a "right" to sex and "freedom" to explore.

The following web site contains much offensive material, but it's important that parents know what their kids are being exposed to and what they are up against. Among the many websites promoting teen sex is <www.teenwire.com> (PPFA), which offers
- how to put on a condom (video)
- how to "come out" as a homosexual
- how to lobby for more sex education in school

In researching this site and others like it, I found nothing encouraging teens to honor their religious values or their upbringing.

1973, and the Planned Parenthood Federation of America's steamroller tactics to normalize the idea of teen sex.

In addition, today's public school students have been fed a steady diet of moral relativism—the idea that there are no moral absolutes and that the worst sin is to judge someone else.

Today, the importance of waiting for marriage for sex, waiting for marriage to live together, and waiting for marriage to have babies has been marginalized as the quaint views of the religious fringe. Christian parents no longer have society on their side when it comes to helping kids navigate the rapids of the teen years. In fact, if you have hopes of your teens maintaining their purity, you must teach them to go against the flow.

And while you're at it, you had better teach them "Don't drink the water," for our kids today travel some polluted streams.

Think about it. In the 1950s Paul and Paula sang about waiting for each other and getting married. The lyrics in that song are strongly contrasted by the message in John Mayer's "Your Body Is a Wonderland," a currently popular, smooth-as-silk paean to no strings attached sex.

Of course, hip-hop and rap lyrics are even harsher. The fast-food attitude toward sex is the reality our teens have to deal with every day.

While songs like yesterday's "When I Fall in Love" or "Goin' to the Chapel" helped reinforce the romantic aspect of boy-girl relationships, they also defined the limits and the goals. It's a clear example of how single-minded our culture was back in the *Father Knows Best* and *Leave It to Beaver* days.

The same sort of corruption that has occurred in music has occurred with television and movies. What would have once been considered pornography is now available for the price of admission or with the click of a remote. I remember from my teenage years a movie called *Splendor in the Grass*, starring Natalie Wood and Warren Beatty. It was groundbreaking in its portrayal of teen sex (in keeping with the times, suggested not shown)—but at the end of the movie, the emphasis was on the great unhappiness that resulted from breaking social taboos.

The switch from romance to eroticism in entertainment has put enormous pressure on today's teens. But it's even more pervasive and subtle than the soft porn now passing for R-rated in movie theaters.

From their youngest years, today's kids have grown up in a culture increasingly obsessed with sex.

When Samantha was growing up in the 1980s, the sexual revolution had made some inroads, to be sure. Some unmarried couples had begun living together; some teenage girls were getting secret prescriptions for the pill. But these were the exception rather than the rule. Culturally, there was still overall agreement about appropriate or moral behavior.

But then the vividly detailed sex lives of national leaders weren't being delivered with the daily news. Victoria's Secret and Herbal Essence commercials didn't assault our visual and auditory senses during TV prime time. Pornography wasn't a mouse-click away. And young readers weren't trying out their new word analysis skills with *Cosmopolitan* and *Redbook* in the checkout line.

Even the most permissive parents would never have dreamed of letting their daughters dress in a sexually provocative way. And our daughters couldn't have found such clothing in kid sizes anyway. Now, any ten-year-old who wants to can dress like an MTV video performer, and for today's parents, the more difficult task is helping their daughters find clothing that doesn't send the wrong message.

It doesn't hurt to stop and take a look at how things really are. Like the proverbial frog in the frying pan, we adults also exist in a culture constantly pushing the limits toward the more permissive and the more sensational. Consider the 2004 Super Bowl halftime show with Justin Timberlake and Janet Jackson. It wasn't just the "wardrobe malfunction" that was shocking, though the outrage was directed there because it was the final shock in an extremely vulgar and decadent dance number foisted on millions of unsuspecting families at halftime.

My second reason for looking back to the way things were is this: because my oldest child is 35, yet I still have 'tweens and teens at home, I've had to grow as a parent myself to meet the extra challenges the younger siblings face each day. I know firsthand that today's cultural climate calls for a little more when it comes to raising teens. As a parent, you just can't count on your culture to back you anymore. You need to take a proactive approach.

This means that in addition to setting clear limits, you need to equip your teens to avoid temptation.

You may need to rethink dating, because dating for two kids who grew up listening to the Shirelles in the 1960s was different than it was for two kids who grew up listening to Bon Jovi in the 1980s.

And dating for two kids who are growing up listening to Eminem and Justin Timberlake—and who have been indoctrinated through the media and sometimes the school with the idea that sex is great and why not go for it—deserves some careful consideration.

What Does God Say?

Discipline your son, and he will give you peace;
he will bring delight to your soul (Prov. 29:17).

No temptation has seized you except what is common to man.
And God is faithful; he will not let you be tempted beyond what
you can bear. But when you are tempted, he will also provide a
way out so that you can stand up under it (1 Cor. 10:13).

The thing all three couples have in common is their hormones. God chose to make the sexual urge a powerful one, all the better to bond a husband and wife in marriage. Every teen has to deal with that reality.

But the 1960s couple had the backing of their families, schools, churches, and communities to draw the line and hold it. They might spend some time alone in a car and kiss or make out, but there was a powerful taboo against "going all the way."

The 1980s couple had it a little bit tougher as, during this time of social transition, they received competing messages from the culture.

But for today's teen couples in a sex-saturated society, the combination of hormones and license makes temptation a much more formidable reality.

Though there are other temptations, I've focused on sex in this chapter because it's where our children need the most support. If our culture were as consistent and adamant about the dangers of teen sex—not just physical, but psychological and emotional—as it is about the dangers of cigarettes, drugs, and alcohol, parents might be able to relax a little.

But it's not, and we can't.

Say you've taken a proactive approach with your teen regarding purity, and you're sure he or she is committed to waiting until marriage. Setting limits is just the beginning. Now you need to equip your teen to avoid temptation.

Here are some ideas that work:

Postpone dating for as long as possible

Some kids are dating by sixth or seventh grade. But no matter how many parents are supporting their kids in these budding relationships, and no matter how cute and innocent they seem, it's wise to discourage them.

The sixth-grade son of a friend of mine told his mom that three girls liked him and were demanding that he choose one to "go with." One girl called him and asked him to meet her at the movies on Saturday. When Tyler told his mom about what would have been his first date, she simply said, "Son, I don't think you need to be thinking about that right now."

"You're right, Mom," he said, looking relieved.

As someone who's already navigated the teen years with two girls and two boys—and is still helping a few more learn to paddle—I've observed that some girls are very pushy about nailing down these relationships with members of the opposite sex, calling frequently, and going public as a couple. I advise my sons not to go that route and to steer clear of kids who do.

The truth is, there's so much more developmentally that needs to be going on with kids this age—like finding their way around in a larger and more densely populated school, figuring out how to deal with five or six teachers with different personalities, building good study habits, bonding with friends, developing compassion—not to mention building a relationship with God. Although there's an increasing interest in the opposite sex, focusing a lot of energy on it can sidetrack a 'tween from some of the more important work that needs to be going on.

Then there are the cold, hard facts I cited in the last chapter: early dating leads to earlier sex. Period.

Support friendships with kids from like-minded families

My five kids aged 15 to 21 have all confirmed that the middle school years represent a fork in the road, for it's during those years that most kids decide which path they're going to take—whether they'll stick with their faith and family values or go their own way.

My older boys homeschooled until ninth grade, so they skipped those years. My daughter Sophia was the first to enter middle school when we moved to Virginia two years ago. Now in ninth grade, Sophia has two very best friends who reinforce her beliefs and values. The three girls are part of a larger circle of "good" girls—pretty, athletically or musically or artistically talented girls who work hard, get good grades, and aren't "boy crazy."

They also attend one or two girls' Bible studies during the week.

Though the popular crowd is dating, they seem content to wait and are having a lot of fun as they do.

My 11-year-old daughter, Madeleine, entered middle school as a sixth-grader this year. Because I learned from observing Sophia how important her support circle was in establishing her confidence in who she is, over the past two years I've tried to dig a little deeper into the values and vision of the parents of Maddy's friends to find out where they stand on issues like early dating. Although it helps to know a family attends church, I've learned that doesn't necessarily mean you share the same approach.

I ask a lot of questions.

Maddy has some friends who will probably be on a different path by the time they get to high school. Even now, some of her elementary friends are slipping away, in a hurry to grow up. That's OK. I want to encourage her friendships with kids who will help her stick to the values she's been brought up with.

Encourage group dates

I'm not living in la-la land. Even as we discuss ways to help your teen keep life balanced, teens need time with members of the opposite sex to learn how to feel comfortable and be friends. And there's the reality that they will develop crushes on each other. Any grown-up knows this is true because we did ourselves.

Often, someone's crush—or several—will generate a group date. A bunch of kids will go to the movies or bowling or out to eat. Though there may be some undercurrent of who likes whom, a group date is a very safe way to give your teen some significant social time without the risks of one-on-one dating.

Be hospitable

Let your home be known as a great place for teens to hang out. Simply put, when your kids invite their friends to your house, you know what's going on. That's worth any extra work you may put in.

For some years, we had a breakfast night each week, with

Dad in charge of serving pancakes, eggs, bacon, sausage, and orange juice. Since many families are too busy to eat big breakfasts these days, and because of the novelty of breakfast food after dark, kids loved to come over for this. I've also heard of families having taco nights or pizza nights.

Seeing your kids' friends on a regular basis is a great way to really get to know them. And someday that might make a difference in their lives.

Give your teen a cell phone

Cell phones are an essential part of today's parenting. Your kids need to know that they can reach you at any time. And you need to know you can reach them.

I remind my kids to take their cell phones with them when they leave the house, to remember to turn them off during movies and turn them back on afterwards, and to check for messages.

Keep your teen accountable for destinations and timetables

In our family, we're all accountable to other members of the family for where we are. My kids need to know where Mom and Dad are, and we need to know where our kids are.

When my kids are going to a party, I call to make sure the parents will be home. I give my kids a curfew—although Virginia, where I live, makes it easy because drivers under 18 can't drive after midnight. And my kids know that if they leave one place for another, they must call home.

Limit time alone with a member of the opposite sex

Our rule is that our kids cannot go into someone's house unless the parents are home. And they can't have someone over unless their dad is at home or I'm at home. As they've gotten older, we've made exceptions for friends of the same sex but never of the opposite sex.

Their bedrooms are off limits to friends of the opposite sex.

Cars can be risky territory, as anyone who's ever been a

teenager knows. When our teens have gone out on dates alone —at 16 or 17—their dad and I remind them to limit their time in the car to getting where they need to go and coming home again.

Eliminate latchkey hours

Long before there was a name for it, I was a latchkey kid. And, I regret to say, during the early 1980s my own two daughters were latchkey kids as well. Looking back, I regret that I ever put them in harm's way.

Today there are approximately seven million latchkey kids in the United States. Research shows that they're more likely to skip school, make lower grades, have sex, get into trouble, and abuse drugs than those coming home to some kind of supervision or to an after-school program.

While many moms plan to stay home during the preschool years, thinking it's OK to work when the kids are older, the truth is that their continued presence in the home—at least during after-school hours—can be of enormous benefit to kids.

If it's necessary in your family that both parents work, try to avoid your children's coming home to an empty house. Talk to your employer about staggering your hours—perhaps one parent can go to work earlier and come home earlier. Or find other parents in a similar situation and team up to provide supervision by forming a co-op, with one parent taking off an afternoon each week or pooling resources to hire supervision for your group.

The goal is to provide the best possible safety and security for your children.

Monitor entertainment

A recent study found that teens who watch sexually oriented television shows are more likely to engage in sex themselves —even if the content consists only of innuendo. *USA Today* reported on a study by psychologist Rebecca Collins that was published in the *Pediatrics* online journal.

Kids who said they watched more sex-oriented pro-
grams at the beginning of the year were more likely than
others their age to become sexually active during the next
year. Those in the top 10% for viewing of sexually related
scenes were twice as likely to engage in intercourse as those
in the lowest 10%, Collins says. The more sex-oriented
scenes they saw, the more likely they were to become sexually active.

"It's social learning: 'monkey see, monkey do,'" Collins says.
"If everyone's talking about sex or having it, and something bad
hardly ever comes out of it, because it doesn't on TV, then they
think, 'Hey, the whole world's doing it, and I need to'" (Marilyn
Elias, "TV Might Rush Teens Into Sex," *USA Today*, September-
ber 6, 2004), <http://www.usatoday.com/news/health/2004
09 06 teens tv sex usat_x.htm>.

That certainly makes sense, doesn't it? After all, advertisers
spend hundreds of thousands of dollars for product placement
—from the Reese's Pieces that were intrinsic to the plot of E.T.
to the Coca-Cola constantly sipped by judges Simon Crowell,
Paula Abdul, and Randy Jackson on *American Idol*.

They know kids imitate what they see on the screen.

So do advocacy groups who holler every time a movie or television star lights up a cigarette. They know seeing celebrities
smoke entices kids to do the same.

Do you see where I'm going with this? If you're a parent
who wants your teens to remain pure until marriage, you need
to monitor their entertainment choices. That means you need
to learn the ins and outs of your television set's, cable's, or
satellite system's operating system. Then you need to block
MTV and other sexually explicit channels.

You need to familiarize yourself with each show or movie
you allow your teen to watch, either by prescreening, watching
it with them, or looking it up at one or more of the numerous
sites set up to equip parents to help their children make good
entertainment choices.

While eventually you'll turn the reins over to them, kids really need a good foundation in this area. They need to know why you're drawing boundaries—what makes you say yes to some things and no to others. This is part of their education in later drawing their own boundaries.

Your children will challenge you. My children challenge me: "Everyone else is seeing it!" Believe me—I know it's hard to be the stick-in-the-mud when other parents seem to let their kids watch anything.

When you've been using the review process for a while to make decisions about movies and TV, your teen will start to review them and say no on his or her own. He or she will also want to push the envelope and see some films of which you don't approve. Be as flexible as you can. It's better for your relationship and—I believe—for your teen's personal walk with God to allow a mistake in this area rather than to be rigid and legalistic.

If you've given your teen a good foundation in choosing entertainment and then have followed up with giving some free-

Get Involved!

When my kids have a hard time taking no for an answer, I say, "OK—let's see what 'ScreenIt!' says." <www.screenit.com> is a movie/DVD review site for parents, with thousands of old and new movie reviews, containing in great detail anything that might be of concern to parents. I especially depend on "ScreenIt!" because since it has no religious or political affiliation, my kids can't argue that the reviewers are just being legalistic.

We sit at the computer together, and I start reading the material under each category out loud: violence, disrespectful attitude, profanities, sex, and so on. More often than not, it's so embarrassing that the discussion is soon over.

Other reliable review places:

Plugged In, a magazine available from Focus on the Family or online at <www.pluggedinonline.com>, covers music (Christian and non), movies, and television shows that appeal specifically to teens. Here you would find that while *Legally Blonde* may have been tolerable, *Legally Blonde II,* under a different director and with a definite pro-homosexual/anti-Christian bias, was a definite no-no. My teens and I read this cover-to-cover each month.

Movieguide, available by subscription or online at <www .movieguide.org>, uses a Christian perspective to analyze a dozen or so movies each month with attention to themes and comparisons with other movies and literature.

I can't emphasize enough that the Motion Picture Association of America (MPAA) rating system does not work for Christian parents. There are some R-rated movies with intelligent, thoughtful material. Some are marred by a gratuitous sex scene (which with forewarning from a source above, you can fast forward), but some are simply realistic battlefield violence in the service of stories that speak to the hearts of boys and men. On the other hand, most PG-13 and many PG movies are full of crass and vulgar language and sexual innuendo.

The Curtis family litmus test: How would it feel to watch it with Jesus sitting beside you?

dom to choose, when he or she makes a mistake, your teen will be less inclined to defensiveness and more open to the direction of the Holy Spirit in future choices.

Safeguard computers

Involvement in online pornography can happen in the very best of families. I know, because it happened in mine.

Six years ago, looking for a site I had visited the day before, I was scrolling through my history and stumbled onto some names of sites I wouldn't have visited in a million years. I clicked on one and was shocked at what I saw.

Now here I was with four teenage sons—and a husband to boot. I gathered them all up and told them what I had found. No one admitted using my computer to visit porn sites. But finally, through checking times, we knew it had to be one particular son. Confronted with the evidence, he lied, then confessed, but said it was the first time it had happened and would never happen again.

Why did I have no filter? Since I had homeschooled my sons, they hadn't had a lot of exposure to worldly stuff, and they were such good boys, I hadn't realized the urgency of the situation.

I was wrong.

For one thing, as a woman, I had no idea how vulnerable all men—even the nicest—are to pornography. One of my biggest regrets is that this blind spot led me to overlook an area where I could have helped my son avoid temptation.

Safeguarding your family means first of all that every mother needs to appreciate how different male sexuality is from female. I "got it" about these differences only through frank discussions with the men in my family following this incident.

And I really "got it" that because males are so much more affected by visual images, the temptation of pornography can be overwhelming.

It's not like the old days when porn was available only at a seedy little store the next town over. Now it's only as far away as the Seven-Eleven or a friend's house, and as near as the computer screen on your desk. While for most women that's not a problem, for most men it is.

Getting serious about helping your teen avoid the temptation of pornography means getting all TV sets and computers out of bedrooms and tucked-away places and into the open.

Teach modesty

Understanding male sexuality is vital for parents of teenage girls. Again, because response to visual stimulation is wired into guys, the way girls dress can create difficulties.

Here's how Brandon, a high school senior from California, put it:

As a Christian guy, I can say with absolute confidence that the way many girls dress today is a stumbling block for me. I understand that girls want to look their best, and I don't disagree with that. But for me as a guy, I can say that looks are not the end-all-be-all to a relationship that a girl might be searching for when she wears those types of clothes.

And Joshua, a college freshman from North Carolina, described the dilemma posed by provocative dress in stark and simple terms: "My earthly self says yes even while my spiritual side says, 'Please stop tempting me.'"

It was my own four sons, now 16 through 21, who first made me aware what a problem it was for them to concentrate in school with girls exposing so much of their bodies. The resulting column I wrote for the *Marin Independent Journal* caused an uproar, though, as parents of girls defended their right to dress the way they wanted and accused me of having the mentality that defended rape "because the victim was asking for it."

That's not the point.

In her excellent book *A Return to Modesty*, Wendy Shalit, a young Jewish college student, describes women as having a natural inclination to modesty. The fact is that in the last two decades there's been a desensitization of girls to this essential part of their nature.

Again, I draw a contrast between the 1980s, when Samantha and her friends—all in the popular crowd—wore their T-shirts over their bathing suits when guys were around. Many girls today, by contrast, revel in the opportunity to bare their bodies, challenging school dress codes (where there are such things) with bare midriffs, short skirts, and thong underwear revealed any time they sit down or bend over.

What message are girls sending when they dress provocatively? I mean, when we see a police officer dressed in a uniform, we know what he or she stands for and what to expect. When we see Target employees in khaki pants and red shirts, we know we can ask them where to find the pots and pans.

Girls need to understand that how we present ourselves—not just in dress but also in speech and conduct—paints a picture of who we are. Women need to be careful about the message they're sending.

In discussing date rape, Shalit says,

Today our society makes fun of modesty, and then we're surprised to find our men behaving abominably. We make fun of virtue, and then are surprised that men's "amorous expressions" often go "farther than virtue may allow" (Wendy Shalit, *A Return to Modesty* [New York: The Free Press/ Simon & Schuster, 1999], 104).

Interestingly, in the uproar over dress codes, several male teachers privately thanked me for addressing what was a problem for them also—men with families at home confronted all day by girls conforming to the message of Victoria's Secret and other similar messages that the main goal in life should be to drive men to distraction.

Teach your daughters to be responsible in this area simply

Discussion Starters

When you see someone in a police uniform, what qualities come to mind? How about a firefighter's uniform? Laboratory coat? Construction boots? Hiking gear? Rodeo costume?

Do we have expectations about people based on how they present themselves?

Do our clothes send a message about who we are? about our intentions—where we're going, what we're doing?

What about the way girls dress? Can that send a message, even one they never intended?

How are boys and girls wired differently? If boys are more visual—as they say they are—aren't they especially vulnerable to skimpy, tight clothing? Do girls have a responsibility not to tempt them to impure thoughts?

by saying no. The other night in the teen department of a local department store, I ran into a couple from church. We hadn't been talking long when their daughter appeared at the dressing room door to show them an outfit she was trying on. I was so impressed! Not only her mom but also her dad was part of her wardrobe decision making. And it was clear that they had standards they would not be persuaded to abandon.

In our home, all it took was Sophia coming down to the kitchen one morning in a pair of jeans with cutouts up the side. Her four older brothers said so—"What do you think a guy thinks when he sees that?"—loud and clear. Girls in our family wear one-piece bathing suits and don't show their midriffs (or midrift, as my youngest daughter Maddy calls it). That's where we've drawn the line. And once the line was drawn, with an explanation that lets them know it's based on our love and desire to protect them, it was easy to maintain it.

Teach strategies

There's no way we can completely insure our children will

What Does God Say?

Word pictures are powerful teaching tools. Here's one I taught my children early on:

> Like a city whose walls are broken down
> is a man who lacks self-control (Prov. 25:28).

Ancient cities had walls to keep out enemies. Any break in the wall made the city vulnerable to attack. Self-control is our own wall of defense against temptation.

> There is a way that seems right to a man,
> but in the end it leads to death (Prov. 14:12).

A vivid reminder for kids not to bend to peer pressure!

not be tempted, but we can prepare them to flee temptation by teaching them the importance of self-control.

Teach your teens when they find themselves faced with temptation to reach out for help—to call you or to call on God.

The teens I interviewed had very specific ways to avoid temptation or deal with it when it arose unexpectedly:

Question: How do you avoid temptation? Please be specific, thinking of problems like cheating, shoplifting, drugs, alcohol, sex.

Alyse: "You can feel temptation. I immediately know when I'm being tempted. When I get that feeling, I stop and think hard about what I'm doing. Would God like this? Would my parents like this? Sometimes I'm not sure. When I'm not sure, I ask myself, *When I get home, will I freely tell my parents about this incident without hesitating or thinking I may get in trouble for it?* I find it easier to say no to the really bad things like sex, drugs, alcohol, and so on. The smaller things like gossiping, changing plans suddenly, and so on are harder to handle. One time I couldn't decide if what I was doing was wrong or right, so I called my mom and talked to her about it on the phone. She was proud of me for calling and not just going along without thinking."

Brandon: "I try to not get into a situation where I'll be tempted. In some cases, such as in cheating, I just don't let the stone start to roll down the hill. I don't let myself fall into sin the first time, since I know from experience that it's much easier to fall into the rut again once you've dug it for yourself. I also find I can just reach out to God, since I know that when I truly strive to find a connection with Him, all the malicious thoughts shy away in terror from His splendor."

Rachel (pseudonym): "I rebuke it first of all; then I pray that God will give me the strength not to give into it. I've never been tempted as far as sex or shoplifting. I haven't ever given into serious drugs, but I have given into cigarettes on a couple of occasions. Afterwards, I just told my parents and dealt with it with them and with God."

Rachel's response points out the need for our teens to know they can discuss even the most uncomfortable situations with us, counting on us to not "freak out" or respond in a negative manner. If you want your teen to keep talking, you need to keep listening.

One mother told me of a son who came into the kitchen looking distraught. He had somehow accidentally clicked into a porn site and felt awful because he had taken a minute or two to click out.

The mom told me, "It was obvious that he was ashamed, and it was hard for him to tell me, but the Holy Spirit wouldn't let him go until he did. I was so grateful he didn't keep it to himself. That's when sin gains power over us—when it's secret.

"We prayed together. I know he would come to me if it happened again."

What a wise mother! Instead of being angry or disgusted, she let her son know that she recognized he was not a perfect human, that she loved him, and that when it came to fleeing temptation, they were on the same side.

Bottom Line for Parents

- Delay dating.
- Encourage group activities.
- Monitor entertainment.
- Encourage modesty.
- Teach strategies for avoiding and fleeing temptation, including prayer.

4. DEVELOPING COMPASSION

Self-sacrifice

I could tell when Tripp picked up the phone that something was terribly wrong. I was calling from a writers' conference, back in ancient pre-cell days, after waiting for ages in line for one of the four phone booths that served more than 300 people like me—compulsive communicators.

"It's really awful," Tripp said, "Levi died today, and Kim is so mad I'm afraid their family will never speak to ours again."

What? Levi was our California neighbors' prize donkey who hee-hawed in greeting whenever we drove past their driveway to turn into our own. His corral was just on the other side of our fence, so he often helped himself to where he thought the grass was greener.

I said "prize donkey," because Levi *was* one. Each year our neighbor Marr waxed his handlebar moustache, got himself and Levi all gussied up, polished up the buggy, and hauled the whole Olsen family, including wife, Kim, kids, Tanner, Gunner, and Skyler, and—most important—Levi to a big donkey competition, which Levi always won.

Levi dead? Though he wasn't our donkey, his loss would leave a hole in our lives. Through our children's friendships, our families were close. And Levi, with his insistent bray, had won a place in our hearts.

But why would Kim be mad at us?

When Tripp told me, I could hardly believe it. One of our sons (who has quite understandably begged to remain anonymous) then 10 years old, had greeted the news of Levi's demise by jumping up and down and laughing, declaring, "Yea! He's dead! Ha, ha! At least we won't have to listen to his stupid braying anymore!"

Unfortunately, the entire Olsen family heard my son's tasteless, heartless, and completely inexplicable remarks. Kim, whose Portuguese ancestry weighs in when she's crossed, let loose a wail. "I can't believe what I'm hearing!" she yelled as she gathered her family into the house and slammed the front door.

I couldn't believe it either. Here I was, 200 miles away from home and completely at a loss. Tripp had left message after message on the Olsens' answering machine, apologizing. Thank God, Kim picked up the phone when I called, and I was able to convince her that our family loved Levi and we were very, very sorry, and that I didn't know what had gotten into my son but that I was sure he didn't really mean what he said.

Then I called home again to talk to my son. What in the world had he been thinking?

"I was just trying to be funny, Mom," was all he could muster up. Six years later, he still doesn't know what led him to try humor as an antidote to bereavement. But he has really come to see that it doesn't work. And our family has since had a quick way to remind anyone when they weren't measuring up, compassion-wise: "Oh, are you having a Levi moment?"

I share this story for its irony, because to have my son behave in a manner so devoid of compassion was like my worst nightmare. Of course, I know it was his immaturity—as well as the fact that some people who live more in their intellect than in their feelings (as he does) have a hard time navigating emotional rapids.

Still, my son's behavior was a particularly striking blow to me as a mother, because developing compassion in my kids has always been top priority.

Perhaps it's because I grew up poor myself, in a fatherless home at a time when divorce wasn't as prevalent as today. With my mom working two or three jobs to support us—taking buses because we didn't own a car and sometimes ending up the month with only oatmeal to eat—I always felt ashamed and not good enough.

But God uses everything for good. Today I know that those experiences have made me a more compassionate and inclusive person—"compassionate" meaning that I'm sensitive to the pain and needs of others, "inclusive" meaning that I'm convinced that everyone, regardless of race, religion, social class, or physical or mental ability, has something unique and worthwhile to offer.

I'm not tooting my own horn here, just recounting how God used the discomfort and helplessness of my childhood to shape me into a person willing and able to sacrifice to help others. Regretfully, though, I sometimes wonder if I can raise my kids to be compassionate, inclusive, and willing to sacrifice when they're growing up in such comfortable circumstances.

How about you? Do you ever worry about building your kids' character in a culture of plenty? Ever wonder if the deck is stacked against you when times aren't tough enough?

What Does God Say?

Rejoice with those who rejoice; mourn with those who mourn. Live in harmony with one another. Do not be proud, but be willing to associate with people of low position. Do not be conceited (Rom. 12:15-16).

All of you, live in harmony with one another; be sympathetic, love as brothers, be compassionate and humble (1 Pet. 3:8).

I mean, I'm grateful Tripp and I are able to give our children so much I missed, but I'm also painfully aware of how those advantages crowd out the character-building that comes from never being able to take your school clothes, your medicine, or even your next meal for granted.

And it doesn't help that we live in a culture heavily skewed toward entertainment—much of it unhealthy—and based on a "me-first" mentality.

That "me-first" mentality certainly doesn't need to be nurtured to thrive. From the get-go, we humans are completely selfish. Starry-eyed parents who think their firstborn will be perfect are taken by surprise the first time they see their little darling ruthlessly wrestle something away from another child.

But why be surprised? That's our natural state. And unfortunately, some people don't get far beyond that either. Our culture does everything it can to feed our mistaken notion that we're the center of the universe—encouraging us to believe that if we have this car or that pair of sneakers, we'll realize our potential. Emblematic of the self-centered mind-set pervasive in our consumer-driven society are advertising slogans like "You deserve a break today" and "Have it your way."

By contrast, the first four words of Rick Warren's phenomenal bestseller, *The Purpose-Driven Life*, say simply, "It's not about you."

Here's where the conflict for our children's hearts and minds is engaged—between the secular, consumer-oriented worldview, which pushes them this way and that way by appealing to their self-centeredness, and our Christian worldview, which teaches that we're here to love and serve God and neighbor, to think more highly of others than ourselves, and to give sacrificially.

It's a daily battle, and parents who want to raise kids who will be compassionate, caring, and selfless must be fully engaged.

First, you need to understand the forces contending for your child's soul. There are those who are deeply interested in your teen, not because they want the best for him or her but because they want to sell something. In 2003, according to a study called "Targeting Teen Consumers," prepared by the Newspaper Association of America, young consumers spent over $175 billion dollars on products and services.

For anyone selling anything in North America, teens are a prize target—considering their purchasing power not only now but for all the years to come. Teens make decisions about whether to drink Coke or Pepsi, eat at McDonald's or Burger King, dress in American Eagle or Abercrombie & Fitch. These companies have studied the markets well, and through their advertising their brand, it becomes associated with a lifestyle or an attitude, so as the teen chooses, he or she becomes personally identified with a certain brand. Drinking Dr. Pepper or eating Pringles can become a statement of who you are.

Remember the good old days when being appropriately dressed meant making sure your labels were tucked inside your clothes? What a brilliant strategy it was when clothing manu-

 Get Involved!

How do the media and marketers regard your teens? For a heavy dose of reality and a few chills, spend some time at the following web sites:

The Merchants of Cool
<http://www.pbs.org/wgbh/pages/frontline/shows/cool>
An online PBS report on the creators and marketers of popular culture for teenagers.

Media Awareness Network
<http://www.media-awareness.ca/english/index.cfm>
(Click on "parents," then "marketing and consumerism.") A Canadian site that helps parents and teachers equip kids with critical thinking skills to understand how the media works and to make intelligent decisions.

facturers persuaded consumers there was status to be found in prominently displaying the name of the manufacturer—sometimes in six-inch letters on T-shirts and sweatshirts—thus reinforcing the self-concept of the brand-identified wearer even while *providing free advertising space!*

Question: What about the peer pressure to have certain things—is that difficult for you? Do you feel you have less than others? How does your faith impact the drive for consumerism? Have your parents done anything to help you in this area?

Kristen: "There's a lot of pressure in teenage culture to have the right things, especially clothes and electronics. Sometimes I felt left out just because I wasn't wearing the right brand of jeans, even though I knew my jeans cost half as much and would last twice as long as theirs. I made it a policy not to go in the "popular" stores like Abercrombie & Fitch and Hollister, because I didn't want to waste my money in pursuit of superficial popularity, nor did I want to support these companies and their blatantly sexual advertising. I feel I have less than others sometimes, especially at my private college where many students own BMWs and fly home regularly, but it doesn't bother me anymore. I don't want more stuff. My parents didn't buy me the "popular" items, and I wasn't spoiled, but I never went too long without something I sincerely wanted. I think the key to biblical consumerism is to examine your motives for buying and see if they align with God's Word. Also, it's good to wait a while before buying something, especially if you're an impulse buyer like me."

Matt, public school graduate, currently a freshman at the University of Missouri at Kansas City: "There's a lot of pressure to have certain things, and I was influenced by that in junior high and the beginning of high school. I think once I really embraced the scripture in Matt. 6—"Where your treasure is, there your heart will be also"—I realized that it wasn't that important to have a bunch of useless stuff; so much of it was fads. I don't really feel I have less then others, and maybe I do in the sense of materialism, but I just try to appreciate the things I *do* have and not take them for granted."

Alyse: "I must say that I don't have much trouble at all with how many things I have and how many things other people have. To be honest with you, I don't understand why so many people feel they have to have the same stuff other people have and look the same way other people look. When I look at society, it makes me sad. It seems to me that all the teenagers have to try to look like all the other teenagers. All the stars have to look like all the other stars, and all the singers have to look like all the other singers. I feel you need to be who God made you to be."

Josh: "Having things in the teenage life does mean a little. Some say it doesn't affect them, but I think it does. But in many other countries, people who have a lot less than us are much happier. I think those who want more are fooling themselves. Those who have a lot still think they need more, making it a never-ending circle that will cause destruction. But as Christians, we aren't of the earthly world, and as hard as it is, we should care nothing about the earthly possessions. My parents did something really helpful. First, they showed me how happy others are with much less by taking me on mission trips to places where the people are less fortunate by earthly standards. They also didn't give me everything I wanted."

Parents can counter the pressure of consumerism on their teens by helping them understand how susceptible we are to advertising. Take product placement, for instance. Type the words "product placement" in Google, and you'll find a heap of information. Product placement began in 1982 when the movie *E.T.* portrayed the irresistible little alien following a trail of Reese's Pieces. Sales for the candy shot up immediately.

Now it's a rare film that doesn't add cash to its coffers with product placement contracts for everything from Huggies diapers to Starbucks coffee to DeLorean dream cars. Rates are structured depending on how the product appears. A can of Coke sitting on a table might cost the Coca-Cola Company a certain amount, but if Tom Cruise picks it up and opens it, it costs a whole lot more. And if he actually brings it to his lips—well, you can imagine!

The more our kids know about the inner workings of the advertising world, the less susceptible they will be to such subliminal manipulation.

Even if you have the money to buy your child everything he or she wants, it's really not the loving thing to do. Teens can't learn to control their impulses for more, more, more if we say yes, yes, yes. How can someone learn to be selfless if his or her attention is riveted on the next thing he or she wants?

 Discussion Starters

Question: When it comes to TV, what is the product being sold? Who is the customer?

Your teens probably think as they watch TV that they're the customer and that the ads they watch display the products being sold.

Not so! For television networks, the customers they serve are the advertisers. The product being sold is the viewer. That's why the cost for a commercial can vary from $19 for a 30-second daytime spot on a local cable channel to $2,000,000 for the same amount of time during the Super Bowl, which attracts the largest television audience every year. The price paid by customer/advertiser is based on the number of viewers during that time slot—the same way we buy meat by the pound.

Encourage your kids to look at commercials with a critical eye, identifying what factors underlie the message: guilt, greed, manipulation, fear, flattery, status-seeking.

It's good for kids to work for things they want. While it's easy to spend Mom and Dad's money, having things come easily doesn't produce good character or a realistic outlook on life.

Take cars, for example. When we lived in Marin County, California, the school parking lots were filled with BMWs and Mercedes Benz—many of them gifts from parents for a 16th birthday. I'm not kidding.

When Josh got his license, his grandma wanted to give him her '80s Jeep Cherokee, but we asked her instead to sell it to him for $500, thinking it was better for him to have something invested in his own car. After a while he saved up and bought himself a newer truck, but in five years since he got his license and his first car, he's never had an accident.

By contrast, I know a talented college freshman who received a brand-new little convertible last year from her divorced father as a gift—and she had three accidents in the first month. Does that prove anything? Well, not exactly. But I can't help wondering if she might have learned from the first accident if she had been required to pay for the car and her own repairs.

What I'm getting at here is that parents need to be creative in trying to tame the consumer consciousness surrounding and being encouraged in our kids. The first—and most essential— aspect of developing compassion is to get their minds off themselves and the things they want for themselves.

The second aspect (and both go on simultaneously) is to guide their attention to others, to prepare their hearts to serve, and to help them discover the joy of generosity.

Teaching kids to think of others and preparing their hearts to serve begins at home. In other times and places this was not a problem at all. In other countries or rural parts of our own—as well as in our own country's history—children have worked together alongside their parents before and after school. In today's homeschooling families, work isn't even compartmentalized but is woven through the other, formal subjects kids are learning.

Still, in general, today's families are smaller and more afflu-
ent and less in need of teamwork. In many homes, as noted on
the latest reality TV shows—*Trading Spouses* and *Wife Swap*—
where contrasting moms are traded for two weeks, there are
many families where Mom runs the house on her own, allowing
the kids to just kick back and enjoy the results. Indeed, this
phenomenon of parents requiring little work from their children has been well-reported recently.

In a big family like mine that was never an option. I always
needed my kids' help and raised them to be part of a team. But
even if I hadn't, I would have required them to help, because I
knew from my Montessori training that this was best for them
—best in terms of developing their work ethic.

As a Christian mother, though, I know there's more than a
work ethic at stake. There's also the path to righteousness we
follow that leads us to follow Christ's example.

So, by all means, if you haven't been requiring much of
your teens at home, it's not too late to start. Just keep in mind
what we discussed in chapter 3, that to avoid resistance, we
need to explain our reasoning to our teens. So a parent might
say, "You know, Jamie, we haven't been requiring many chores
from you, and all of a sudden I've realized we're not doing you
any favors by that, because that's not good preparation for
when you have roommates or a family of your own. So here's
the new plan. . . ."

Earning money is also good, because even though the work
involves pay, it means our teens are serving. So encourage your
teens to get jobs. That has the added advantage of making sure
their time is spent doing something productive rather than
hours of watch TV or playing video games.

And then, of course, there's volunteerism, which in recent
years has become downright trendy. In our communities there
are many ways to serve and many people who need help. All it
takes is the willingness. And the more we serve others, the less
we'll be thinking of ourselves.

Get Involved!

There's a familiar old expression that goes, "Your actions speak so loudly that I can't hear what you're saying." The truth is, the best way for parents to build their teens' compassion is to model it themselves.

Here are some ways parents can lead their children into demonstrating compassion.

- Volunteer for church outreaches.
- Work with Special Olympics.
- Baby-sit for single mothers.
- Invite single mothers and their children to church activities.
- Do lawn work for elderly neighbors.
- Visit, read to, or sing for the elderly, shut-ins, or hospitalized kids.
- Minister to and feed the homeless.
- Serve at a food bank or soup kitchen.
- Sponsor a child through World Vision or another similar program.
- Provide foster care.
- Adopt a child or sibling group at home or abroad.

A popular slogan today is "Live locally—think globally." I would like to see the Christian community make this slogan our own so that our teens are not only making mission trips—which I think are very worthwhile for startling them into an awareness of our advantages—but are also engaging themselves at home where there are needs and learning how to relate in a Christlike manner to those with whom the Church seems often at odds.

Yes, I know we all say, "Hate the sin and love the sinner." I just don't know how much experience most of us adults have in living this out. We're still seeing grown-up Christian men in leadership positions carrying signs saying, "God hates fags."

Our children, on the other hand, are confronted with homosexuality on a daily basis—and not just in the liberal-leaning metropolitan areas of the "blue states." They have gay teachers, choir directors, and classmates.

While some teens have learned to deal with it and may have a few helpful ideas for their parents, others struggle with the issue of how to apply the principle of hating the sin and loving the sinner into their daily lives. Listen to this range of responses:

Question: How should faithful Christians act toward gays?

Josh: "Christians are not to judge others, so we should not judge those who are gay. Although their lifestyle is not right, we should be friends with them anyway. They really are great people, just as we are. Gay marriage is something totally different. I don't believe that gays should marry and raise children, because it would be detrimental to the children."

Amy: "Gays are a hard subject. There are gays in my school, and everyone acts outwardly cool to them, but you can tell that on the inside people tend to shy away from them. They get picked on quite a bit, I've noticed—especially when a straight guy is around a gay guy. Some of the things I've heard the wrestlers at my school say about this one gay guy are brutal. It's hard for Christians to be friends with gays, especially when the gay guy says he's a Christian and goes to church—but yet still talks about guys that he likes. It's confusing a little. I'm not sure what to think about the validity of his claim of being Christian—but then again, sin is sin, and I'm not perfect either."

Alyse: "I believe Christians should not shun gay people but treat them nicely, as we're supposed to, while not encouraging their behavior. I would not become very close to a gay or lesbian, because I don't want to be close to someone I feel is going against what the Bible teaches. I would never treat a gay person badly, but I would let the person know that I don't agree with his or her lifestyle."

Matt: "I feel that Christians should accept gays, even if it means tolerating their lifestyle. However, that doesn't mean we have to support it. We should try to teach them through love and kindness, not ridicule and judgment."

Kristen: "I honestly don't think Jesus would be whacking homosexuals over the head with a picket sign. Rather, He would talk with them and show that He cared about them without supporting their lifestyle."

Another problematic area for Christians now is multiculturalism. Some would say we live in a post-Christian society. While that's certainly not true in sheer numbers of populace (most Americans still identify themselves as Christians), it's true in terms of the pluralistic attitude we're supposed to have —as though all religions were equally valid. Our position with regard to Islamics now is conflicted as we hear some of them say they feel theirs is a religion of peace even while radical Islamics plot against Christians.

These are examples of areas in which we need to trust God and teach our children to trust Him as well. My teens are frequently working side-by-side with homosexuals, because they're involved in theater. While some Christians might not allow their teens to be involved in entertaining or performing because of this, I look at it as a chance to let our family's light shine. After all, we might be the only Christians some of these people know. And I remember how Jesus hung out with the social misfits of His time—the prostitutes, the tax collectors— how He spoke to the woman at the well who had had five husbands. The best we can do, I believe, is to follow His example.

As far as thinking globally, magazines like *National Geographic* and *World Vision* provide excellent visual reminders that Americans enjoy privileges and abundance that should compel us to share. In an effort to keep my kids from taking for granted what they have, I cut out the most poignant pictures and hang them up throughout the house.

For Christian teens, mission trips can open their eyes to the

What Does God Say?

As God's chosen people, holy and dearly loved, clothe yourselves with compassion, kindness, humility, gentleness and patience (Col. 3:12-15).

A generous man will prosper; he who refreshes others will himself be refreshed (Prov. 11:25).

reality faced by most people throughout the world. I remember when Jasmine first went on a short-term mission to Mexico, she came back a changed teen. "Mom, this one family's house had a dirt floor and was only as big as our living room. There were five children, and one had some sort of handicap, just sitting in the corner watching his mother. She was so thrilled we were visiting their village—she killed two chickens and invited us for dinner. And she was so eager to share!"

Amy likewise felt changed: "This summer I went to Denver. It was very much an eye-opener. We worked primarily with the homeless and lower-income Hispanic families in the Denver area. A large percentage (probably 80 or more) of the area we were in was Hispanic. All the signs on buildings were in Spanish, and that's what everyone spoke in the neighborhoods. I was especially touched while working with the Mexican children at the church where we were staying. Some spoke no English at all. The older kids—around 9 or 10, sometimes younger—translated for the younger kids. They were so sweet and innocent, and it was obvious that the parents were trying hard to make a good life for their kids. Most of the older ones who spoke English moved to the states from Mexico when they were around five or so. They told me about what they liked to do, their friends. We colored pictures, and they were just like

American children, only somewhat mentally older than they should have been. It changed how I look at Hispanics. They are just trying to get through this life like everyone else, and they come to the church because they know they can depend on it to provide food and clothing. It's also a good outreach for the church to show God to people. They have a small church service before handing out the food and clothes each day."

And Josh: "I've done quite a few missions. I've done two missions with an organization called Appalachian Service Project. And it really has opened my eyes to other people in the world. The one that changed me drastically was my trip to

Discussion Starters

As I was writing this chapter, the tsunami in southeast Asia occurred, on December 26, 2004, killing hundreds of thousands and leaving many times more without homes or families. Perhaps it was the timing that made it even more staggering. The contrast between our comfy Christmas and the devastation on the other side of the globe hurt my heart. Would you understand if I said I wanted it to hurt my children's hearts too?

At times like this, here's my advice for parents:

- Do all you can to manage the meaning of a disaster in a way that will build your kids' character, compassion, and willingness to sacrifice for those in need.
- Watch the media coverage with them.
- Check the location on the globe. Look up information on the politics, religion, and conflicts of the country.
- Teach your teens to give intelligently to legitimate venues.
- Teach them to give sacrificially, giving up something in order to donate.
- Read or tell stories of survivors—to instill a message of hope.
- Look for stories of courage and selflessness, like vacationers who after the tsunami rolled up their sleeves and went to work helping wherever they could.

China. I made some great friends, and I learned to spread the Word and realized that we have many advantages we take for granted in America. I just finished writing an e-mail to a friend I made in China. It allowed me to see the world in a bigger sense. Yes, my family does support missionaries. The church that we're a part of—wherever my dad may be placed—supports a family that goes to India, Brazil, and many other countries. I think it's great that World Vision and other organizations exist. It's one thing to be poor. It's another not to be able to support a child."

Question: How have your parents helped you develop compassion?

Amy: "My mom always gave me the last cookie in the box. It's always been those little sacrifices that mean the most to me. Also, my mom and I have adopted two little girls—one through World Vision and one through the God's Child Project. It's neat to hear from them and know that it's changing someone's life."

Jack: "My dad makes a lot of money, but he's always been very free with it. Everyone who comes to the door selling stuff makes a sale. He's even developed a reputation. One day a kid came by, and my mom thanked him but told him we weren't interested. Then he asked if Dad was home."

Joanna: "My dad always puts everyone else before himself. We have six cars in our family, and dad drives the old clunker—just because he loves seeing us enjoy the nice things. He'll save up his money during the week just so we can all go out to eat, just because he knows we all love to. He hasn't bought new clothes in about 15 years, just so his kids can have nice things."

Michael: "My dad would take us downtown and talk to the homeless. They would ask for a dollar, and he would take them out to eat, talk to them. When a new church was starting in our community, we went and painted walls for them."

Matt: "My mom helped me develop compassion by taking me

to school with her twice a year. She's an early-childhood special education teacher, which requires a lot of compassion. At the beginning of the day I would dread it and have no patience, but by the end I really cared for the kids. I feel it's important for parents to show compassion to their children and even to others, be it strangers or family. They set the example whether they want to or not."

On a personal level, I understand that it doesn't come naturally to have compassion for people who are different. Most of the time, it takes a conscious effort. I know my life changed when my eighth child, Jonny, was born with Down syndrome in 1993. As we explored this new terrain, meeting people with all sorts of disabilities, I realized how aloof I had been from that world. It wasn't as though I didn't care; it was more as though I were oblivious. Now, through my son, I was a member of this community. Since then, members of my family, who might never have sought out such positions, have taught Sunday School, coached teams, and staffed summer camps for kids with disabilities—not to mention that we adopted three more boys with Down syndrome. Through Jonny, God opened up a whole new world of service to us.

Likewise, after Matt's mother took him out of his comfort zone to let him rub elbows with kids who were a little different, Matt made her compassion his own. Listen to this story he shared with me:

There was this handicapped kid in my Spanish class whom no one really paid much attention to. They would talk behind his back and pretty much ignored him. I honestly didn't think too much of him at first either. Well, it came time to partner up with people (we did that a lot in Spanish), and I ended up with him. I realized he was into sports, especially baseball, (which I'm not a big fan of), so we talked a lot of sports. He really started to open up and asked if he could be my partner again when we matched up. To make a long story short, I continued working with him.

Eventually I got called to stay after class by my teacher. At first I was trying to figure out what I did to get in trouble. She ended up telling me how much she admired my kindness and compassion towards Ryan. I didn't think it was that big of a deal, but she started crying and said that his grades were up significantly. She made me realize the impact we can have on someone's life just through compassion and the ripple effect it has.

 Bottom Line for Parents

- Emphasize Rick Warren's words: "It's not about you."
- Build your teen's resistance to peer pressure.
- Educate/inoculate your teen against media manipulation.
- Limit spending on *things*.
- Help individuals in your community.
- Support those in need around the world.
- Stretch your family's comfort zone.

Self-respect

I wonder whether a couple years ago I would have included standing up for what's right as one of the seven basics with which parents need to equip teens. Until the dirty dancing at the prom issue came up in my teens' lives, and the subsequent conversations I had later with other teens, I don't think I understood how much on the frontlines our kids are each day.

The fact is that good kids have to put up with a lot of bad stuff every day—verbal and sometimes even physical abuse from kids who aren't being raised with respect for authority or their peers, kids who consequently have no self-respect and whose own pain drives them to lash out at anyone they consider weaker.

When we first moved to Virginia in 2002, three of my sons entered public high school for the first time after years of home and Christian schooling. Coming from California, I was delighted at the quality of public schools in Loudoun County. The Virginia legislature had recently mandated that "In God We Trust" be posted in school hallways, even as our former state was removing "one nation under God" from the Pledge of Allegiance. While in Marin County only four percent of the population attended church, and Christian teachers were about as scarce as they could be. In Virginia we saw principals and teachers in the very first churches we visited.

Our high school serves 1,200 kids from the rural portion of

the county and is located in the largest town (population less than 4,000). It's the kind of place you see in movies—no movie theater of its own, only three franchise food places, two stoplights, and one big water tower looming across the street from the high school, the perfect place for emblazoning the name of the school team: the Vikings.

Western Loudoun has been the kind of place populated by more traditional, stable families, where families have known each other for generations, where teachers are teaching children of former students, and where the entire town turns out for football and basketball games. As a matter of fact, all eyes are always on whatever's happening at the high school—sports, homecoming, prom, graduation.

But the demographics of our county are changing as the urban is sprawling toward us from the east, and Loudoun was recently named the fastest-growing county in the United States. The schools to the east are clearly feeling the effects in terms of gangs, bullying, and the threat of vandalism and violence. But a patchwork of zoning ordinances has kept our little corner of the world somewhat more protected. Our high school has always enjoyed a reputation of being a "good" student body.

But no matter how "good" the reputation of the student body is, good kids in public school are still exposed to a lot of injustice, and Christian kids face persecution for their faith from teachers and peers. I've heard enough to know they need to be encouraged and empowered to stand up for what's right for themselves, for others, and for the good of the culture.

Let's start with the little everyday things. Ben's entry into high school was marred by the merciless verbal and physical insults of the jocks (yes, unfortunately, the old hierarchy reigns, in which the football players and cheerleaders still rule the school and there are lots of "nobodies"). Though Ben was a strapping and masculine 6'2", the jocks decided to call him "gay" (since we were from California), "fat" (which he's not), and "duck-footed" (huh?). He also got shoved around. When

Ben told me stuff like this, the she-bear in me wanted to go down and knock down some egos, but the wise momma in me knew that it was not my battle to fight.

One day a few months into the school year, I asked Ben how the conflict was going.

"Oh, don't worry about it, Mom—I took care of it," he said. Then he told me the secret of his success. One day when one of the guys threw a book at him, Ben got so mad that he lobbed it back, hitting the shocked jock right on the head.

Now, mother to mother, I'm guessing some of my readers are feeling uncomfortable with this turn of events. That's because we're women and don't handle things the way men do. I've raised boys long enough to see that my ways don't always work for the kinds of conflict they face, but their ways do. Guys are just different. I might not understand, but I have to respect that.

And it worked. Those guys never bothered Ben again. He learned an important lesson in standing up for what's right, and I learned a lesson from watching him. Sometimes you have to have a showdown. And if you do, you need to be intent on winning.

What Does God Say?

Be strong and courageous. Do not be afraid or terrified because of them, for the LORD your God goes with you; he will never leave you nor forsake you (Deut. 31:6).

I can do everything through him who gives me strength (Phil. 4:13).

God did not give us a spirit of timidity, but a spirit of power, of love and of self-discipline (2 Tim. 1:7).

Question: Have you ever faced a situation in which you felt you had to stand up for what's right? What happened?

Brandon: "Yep. Late middle school—one of my teachers asked the students to go to two opposite sides of the classroom, one side if you were planning on being sexually active before marriage, and the other if you were planning to wait. I chose the side that was for those who were choosing to save themselves for marriage—me and three other friends out of a class of close to 40 students. I got a little bit of grief for it for a couple days after, but then everyone stopped. Yet even to this day they remember that Brandon is going to save himself for his wedding night. And I still won't have it any other way.

"I also tried to start a Christian club at my school at the beginning of my junior year. The club was initially denied by the principal to exist as an official club. After talking with my parents and doing a lot of research, I made an appointment with the superintendent of the school district and explained to her that I just wanted the same rights as those of any other school-sponsored club. My club was allowed the following month.

Alyse: "Yes! Here is just one example. A while ago I went to a birthday party for one of my friends. The girls there decided to act out Jerry Springer. I did not like that idea at all and told them I did not want to do that. They told me that was what they were going to do. When I said that I would go upstairs and read until they were done, they tried to convince me to play with them. I refused and found a book upstairs. The girl's mother talked to me about the incident while the others played. She was proud of me and disappointed in her daughter. I had a great discussion with my friend's mom while the other girls played Jerry Springer."

Gabe (requested pseudonym): "Yeah, a few times. Unfortunately, the first few times I kind of blew it and didn't really stand up for my faith. One time I do remember standing up for

Get Involved!

A few years ago, Sophia's teacher gave this assignment: make holiday posters. She also made it clear: no religion allowed. I guess it wouldn't be Christmas without the fear of a lawsuit, would it?

But this skittishness about religious expression in schools is unfounded. In 1995 United States Secretary of Education Richard Riley issued a remarkably concise, clear, and sensible document titled "Religious Expression in Public Schools: a Statement of Principles" (<http://www.ed.gov/Speeches/08-1995/religion.html>). The guidelines affirm that while teachers may not encourage or join in students' religious activity, the school's official religious neutrality requires that "Teachers and administrators are also prohibited from discouraging activity because of its religious content, and from soliciting or encouraging antireligious activity."

Every Christian family with kids in public schools needs to know its rights. And for help, you can turn to the American Center for Law and Justice, which "is dedicated to protecting your religious and constitutional freedoms." Visit <www.aclj.org>.

my faith was at a party where some guys I knew from high school were teasing this girl about not drinking and how she never bent the rules or anything. Well, it got to the point that they were harassing her pretty bad, so I told the guys to lay off. Of course, they then started teasing me about how I never would have said that before and that I should just mind my own business. They ended up completely forgetting about her and just messing with me. But after a while they realized I wasn't going to budge on my stance, so they left. About two months later, one of the guys in that group, Tyler, told me how he quit drinking and was even going to church with his girlfriend sometimes. He felt bad for what he did, and it was really cool to see him come full circle."

Kristen: "I auditioned for a play in 10th grade. I was cast in a role before I had been able to read the whole play. After I got my script and read through it, though, I became uneasy. My character drank, smoked marijuana, and made out onstage, and there was no repentance or "that's wrong" message at all. The end made the point that you can do whatever you want as long as you feel good about it. We rehearsed for a couple of weeks before I was able to make myself quit. Then my friend, who was playing the lead and also felt uncomfortable with being in this production, quit as well. The play bombed in the end, and I was so glad I had not been a part of such a hedonistic show."

Many Christian kids are drawn to the performing arts. I think it's because so many of them are exceptionally talented. My kids and I watch *American Idol* together. It's remarkable that most of the finalists and all of the winners have been believers. If they haven't mentioned it to begin with—thanking God when they make it through to another round—you see it when they run the biographical sketches with footage of them singing in church. Let's face it—when it comes to singing, Christian kids have a real advantage over others. They grow up singing in Sunday School, worship services, at home with their families. And the flair for drama—well, maybe that begins with listening to all those vivid Bible stories and using their imaginations.

But being involved in theater presents different challenges than those of being involved in sports. A high school football player can enjoy doing what he loves, and then—as Rick revealed earlier—separate himself from extracurricular activities like partying or visiting strip clubs with his teammates. For kids who love to sing and act, however, some plays are just not compatible with their core values.

I'm familiar with the faith/theater conflict, because most of my kids have been or still are actively involved in school plays and community theater. Last summer, Ben and two buddies—Christian and Joel, whom you met in earlier chapters—went "over the mountain" (colorful local lingo for driving west from our county over the Blue Ridge) to West Virginia to audition for a production of *Grease* at the Charles Town Opera House. Christian landed the lead, and Ben and Joel got solo singing parts.

But the thrill of success didn't last too long for Christian. On his first reading of the script, he decided the play was just a little too "sketchy," and he dropped out. Ben quickly followed. Joel stayed on and replaced Christian as the lead.

None judged the other for his decision.

This experience illustrates an important point. Navigating the rough waters of our culture—where decisions like this are concerned—isn't something black and white in which teens and their families can consult a list of predetermined rules. God has His reasons for what He asks from us. I appreciated the fact that though Christian and Ben dropped out of the play, they didn't pressure Joel or judge him for his decision.

This is an area where I believe parents also need to give up control and allow their teens to come to their own conclusions. Will some teens make mistakes in judgment? Yes. Do we adults make mistakes in judgment? Yes. Will the world fall apart if a child of ours is in a "sketchy" play (I use that word because it's a current teen adjective that effectively captures what I mean here —things somewhat questionable but not out-and-out wrong)?

As I pointed out before when discussing why we let Ben pierce his ear way back when good Christian families just weren't allowing that, I think it's important to save saying no for the really big things like drugs and alcohol and sex. When parents say no about a lot of things and don't turn any decision-making over to their teens, they're upping the ante for rebellious thoughts and behavior.

Here's how Kristen explained the role her parents played as she struggled with her theater conflict:

My parents really helped me deal with quitting the show. They read the script as well, and while they did not directly tell me to quit, they did tell me that they didn't like the play itself and explained why, but they left it up to me in the end. After I quit, they told me they were proud of me, and their support really helped me make the right decision.

I think it's important for parents to not directly order their kids to "do the right thing" in situations like that. It meant so much more to me because I made the decision myself. My parents influenced me, of course, but in just telling me what they thought of the play they put the responsibility on me to figure out what to do. It made me behave more maturely I think. When parents order their kids to do or not do something, it makes the teen frustrated and rebellious. Teenagers just want to be treated like adults. While you can't kick them out of the house yet, respect them as adults and let them make some moral decisions on their own. Of course, all of that is dependent on how mature your teenagers are.

Even more than adults, teens who are true to their convictions face ridicule from their peers. And surprisingly, even from kids who claim to be Christians.

Jack, an artistic-looking senior from our Kansas City focus group, described his initial disappointment with Christian school: "My parents put me in a Christian school in 8th grade after being homeschooled for several years. I really didn't fit in with those kids, and they didn't really care about being Christians. A lot of them were bitter because they were there. For the first semester it was awful. I begged my parents to take me out and homeschool me again, but they just kept praying with me and giving me Bible verses to keep me strong. A couple of times my Mom even cried with me. That meant a lot. Second semester was a lot better. By the end of the year those same kids had become my really good friends and all of us had grown in our relationship with Christ.

"If Mom and Dad hadn't forced me to stay, I wouldn't have learned what I needed to in order to survive the things I've faced in high school. That difficult experience has helped shape who I am today."

Notice that Jack's parents, while sympathetic and comforting, remained firm that Jack should be in school. This experience differs from Kristen's parents letting her make a decision on her own because of the age difference and because more was at stake.

As Jack's story reveals, for Christian teens raised to apply their faith and values in their everyday life, confronting bad attitudes among Christian peers can be very disappointing.

Kristen put it this way: "It's interesting to me how sometimes the most forceful pressures can come from your peers in youth group at church. I remember once I was sitting with a bunch of youth, and they were passing notes back and forth during the 'big church' service, and they were not being at all discreet. So finally I got sick of it, and the next time a note was handed to me I tore it up into little pieces and passed it along. Everyone stared at me like I was the biggest dork on the planet, but I had to do something, and I was very glad after I did it."

And Brittany, a homeschooled senior from Indiana who does web design and runs a Christian web site for teens, had this to say: "Yes, I have been confronted about my faith by some of my non-Christian friends. A few of them have mocked my standards and my belief in Christ—but surprisingly, most of them seem to respect my faith. I have had to stand up for my values more times than I can count, sadly, to some of my friends who call themselves Christians.

"I don't want to judge whether or not they are really Christians—that's between them and God. However, they have made different choices than I have. They have chosen to push the line of purity and modesty. And crude and rude jokes flow freely through their conversations. They will sometimes mock me for my stance on purity and modesty and wonder why I don't laugh at their jokes. As kindly as I know how, I explain that I feel convicted by God through the Bible that as a Christian, I need and want to save myself for marriage and I don't want to cause my Christian brothers to stumble by the way I dress or act. It has upset some of them before, and they have accused me of saying that I'm better than them and that I'm being narrow-minded and a prude. It hurts, but through it all I have learned better how to state what I believe without sounding judgmental. One thing I know is that I don't want to back down on my standards, and I don't want to be close-mouthed about it."

Brittany brings up an area where parents can really help their children. We want our kids to have confidence and courage as they stand up for what's right. But we also want to teach them to do it in as winsome a way as possible. Coming across as haughty or self-righteous doesn't change people's hearts and is a terrible witness for faith.

What Does God Say?

Speak up for those who cannot speak for themselves, for the rights of all who are destitute. Speak up and judge fairly; defend the rights of the poor and needy (Prov. 31:8-9).

Be wise in the way you act toward outsiders; make the most of every opportunity. Let your conversation be always full of grace, seasoned with salt, so that you may know how to answer everyone (Col. 4:5-6).

Tripp has always taught our kids this principle: "It's not *who's* right but *what's* right." With that in mind, it's easier to confront wrong in a humbly confident way—as though you were just doing your job standing up for what's right. After all, if you weren't around, God would probably just pick someone else.

It's a mystery to me how so many people can see something terribly wrong going on and not do something about it. Many teens are really only following the lead of their parents when they avoid confrontation. One young woman deeply regretted her parents' not taking a stand where it was needed: "I wish my parents had taken a larger part in keeping the youth pastor and youth group accountable. I was miserable in youth group and eventually stopped going entirely. Nothing we did helped me grow in my walk with Christ—it was all just a social event. Because I didn't fit in with the clique and felt that I couldn't contribute anything to these "pizza and yo-yo" gatherings, I was extremely uncomfortable all the time. Even my youth pastor did nothing to help me feel welcome. I think he thought I was strange for not enjoying the food and games thing. But because there was no one there with whom I felt comfortable, and because it was a social event, I began to have panic attacks at youth group meetings. Not long afterwards, I quit going to youth group, because every time I was there I had a panic attack. But by that time the anxiety had spread to other areas of my life and I began feeling panicky in other places besides youth group. Thanks to God, medication, and Christian therapists, I don't have problems with panic attacks anymore.

"There are a lot of Christians who tell me that if I really had a relationship with God I would not have these problems, and it's all spiritual. I admit that I haven't always trusted God with my life like I should have, but that doesn't mean that all persons who aren't "right" with God have psychological disorders. No one seemed to understand my difficulty or was willing to listen and not condemn me for this experience. In the end, though, I believe that if my church and the parents of the youth in the church had been more involved in the youth group, they would have understood that their children were not learning anything that would help them in the real world and could have helped reform the youth group. Parents should be involved in all aspects of their youth's lives, even church, because most parents are unaware that over half of all born-again Christian youth will abandon their faith within the first year of college and that the youth group may be doing nothing to prevent that from happening."

I'm the opposite, I suppose. When I see something wrong going on, I'm compelled to do what I can to make it right. That's why when Ben and Zach told me about the dirty dancing that had been going on at school dances, I immediately wrote a letter to the principal and the school board. And I used my column space to give parents a heads-up.

Some parents were grateful; some parents were mad. They seemed to think that because we had a school that enjoyed the reputation of "good" kids and a principal with a reputation for good discipline, I must be making this up. Yes, the kids were "good" kids with big hearts—as evidenced when they voted a classmate with Down syndrome homecoming queen this year—but that didn't mean they were above reproach. Yes, the principal had a good history of discipline, but he had been confined to a wheelchair for some years and had died that fall.

Besides, according to the students I talked to, the chaperones congregated together and did little active chaperoning, which is defined as "supervising behavior." The room was very dark, and the worst dancing was in the center of the dance floor, an area the adults avoided. Many kids were so offended by what they referred to as "simulated sex" that they just stopped going to school dances. According to graduates of the school, this had been going on for years.

Apparently I was the first person to start making a fuss about it. Even while denying there was a problem at all, the new principal assured me that he had a handle on the situation for the prom.

Though Zach and Ben didn't go to the prom, my oldest son, Josh, went with his girlfriend. When I asked him how things had gone, he said the dancing was worse than ever. So much for the new principal's handle on the situation.

And there were individual stories that made it worse—a

sweet, Christian girl we knew had given in to peer pressure and was freak dancing with her date. Another didn't give in, and her date ditched her. I wondered how many girls felt remorse the day after the prom.

Clearly, adults had completely abnegated their responsibility.

Into this leadership void came a then 17-year-old junior—my sons' friend Christian Amonson.

I first met Christian when he biked the mile from his house to introduce himself to the new neighbors from California. He had heard we had teenage boys and quickly became pals with all four of them. Christian always seemed to pop up for dinner when I was serving fish—he says it's a coincidence, but everyone knows it's his favorite food. And the guys did a lot of things together from airsoft wars to Bible studies to musicals.

In fact, it was at rehearsals for a musical that I first saw Christian's natural tendency to take charge. I noticed that when the adults were not keeping order and moving things along, Christian jumped in and started leading.

So it didn't surprise me too much that instead of simply boycotting the prom, Christian responded by setting up an "ante-prom" ("ante" meaning before), held on the eve of the prom. In addition to having problems with the "freak dancing" (or "freaking," as the kids call it), Christian was also concerned about the skyrocketing cost of the prom. He wanted to provide an affordable, wholesome, and fun alternative. He rented a hall, hired a swing band, and printed posters and tickets. Students came and danced the night away and had a good time.

But thinking long-term, Christian wanted to do more than provide an alternative. He wanted to change the dances into the inclusive, fun events they once were. When I told him people could speak publicly at school board meetings, he formed a delegation of about a dozen students and a few parents to attend the next meeting and called to be put on the agenda. Though there were many other kids who objected to the behavior at the dances, not everyone had the courage to speak out publicly. But for those who were on the fence, Christian was very persuasive.

The media got wind of the story and its intriguing angle—that it wasn't parents leading the call for decency, but students. They drove the hour from Washington, D.C., to interview the kids and stand in front of the high school with a microphone for the evening news.

The school board was not thrilled to see so many people show up to ask for its help getting school dances back on track. The board downplayed the delegation's concerns with remarks like "Well, people objected to the tango and the twist when they first came out." They didn't want to hear the movements of the dancing described, nor would they listen to the lyrics of the rap songs because of the obscenities. Ironic, since the students in their district were dancing to them.

In the days that followed, the school administration and board circled the wagons, claiming there was no problem. In the meantime, though, the superintendent called a meeting of high school principals and drafted a contract for future dances. Since our high school's prom was the first, and because Christian acted so quickly, every other school required students and parents to sign a contract, "Dance Rules and Regulations," which stated specifics like "No freak dancing" and "Students must face each other." In addition, it spelled out the disciplinary steps that would result for students who broke the rules.

It's interesting that even as they denied there was a problem, school officials were working behind the scenes to correct it. Reports from other proms indicated big changes: lights remained on, with chaperones, teachers, and school board members mingling among the dancers. Behavior was much more appropriate.

In addition, the following fall a new item appeared in the Student Rights and Responsibilities Handbook, stating that conduct at school dances is governed by the same rules that apply any other time students are under school supervision, that "obscene or provocative dancing is also prohibited" and that students not in compliance would be removed from the dance. The paragraph was almost word-for-word the same as the one presented to the board by Christian on the night he took a stand.

 # Discussion Starters

If a picture says a thousand words, a movie can be worth a million. These three movies are inspiring portraits of people who stood firm:

High Noon, 1952, Gary Cooper, Grace Kelly, Lloyd Bridges
In this landmark Western, a newly married town marshall faces a gang of killers alone. The townspeople, while professing admiration for their hero, refuse to help him rise to their defense. This Oscar-winner offers a powerful portrait of what it means to stand up for good even when those you serve desert you.

To Kill a Mockingbird, 1962, Gregory Peck
In this exquisite movie set in Alabama during the Depression, a widowed, small-town lawyer's quiet life is dramatically changed when he is called upon to defend a Black man accused of raping a white woman. Told through the eyes of his young daughter, we see a compassionate and courageous man take a stand for justice in spite of the persecution he must endure.

Bonhoeffer, 2003
This compelling documentary about the life of Dietrich Bonhoeffer, a Christian theologian who ultimately gave his life in an effort to stop Hitler's tyrannical rule and oppression of the Jewish race, is an inspirational testimony to the fact that God can use one ordinary person to make a difference.

But that wasn't quite the end of the story. In October our high school students had to sign the dance contract in order to go to the homecoming dance. Most were unaware that the fallout from their own prom had resulted in the contracts that other prom-goers had to sign. Now there was a mini-uproar as students—with a lot of support from a mother who thought their civil liberties were being violated—circulated a petition, collecting 300 signatures (out of a student body of 1,200). The media came back for another round and even covered the dance itself.

There were many things the principal could have done to make the most of this teachable moment, but he didn't. He didn't explain to the student body that their taking things to the limit had left little choice but for the adults to lower the boom. He didn't explain that the term "free expression" doesn't mean that you can do anything you like at a school function.

Many kids signed the pledge but attended the dance with an attitude of defiance. Chaperones were more involved, but as soon as they would turn from breaking up one freak dancing couple to remind another, the first would be at it again.

Afterwards another hip mother wrote a letter to the editor of our local paper complaining that her son's experience at the dance was ruined by the chaperones.

A father who had signed up to chaperone because his sophomore daughter had come home crying from the previous year's homecoming, wrote in response:

Were all the students happy with the chaperone arrangements? Probably not. Were chaperones necessary? Clearly they were. Students were asked to pledge that they would abide by certain rules at the dance. Thus, all the students who attended the dance had signed the pledge and therefore given their words that they would comply with the rules. What should be of grave concern to our community is the fact that a number of those students brazenly and defiantly reneged on their promise and engaged in conduct that violated their pledge. Many even did it with an apparent sense of pride. Regardless of one's feelings about "freak dancing," a promise should still be a promise. What are their parents teaching them?

As for the "freak dancing" itself, the parents of the

youth engaged in this dancing must see their sons and daughters engaged in this form of dance before they pass judgment on it. It will shock you. It will disturb you. Fortunately, the great majority of students kept their word. . . . There are those who accuse [a small minority] of imposing their moral standard on others. To this specious argument I would reply that it is more of an imposition to subject the majority of honorable students to the questionable moral conduct of a defiant few. No one has been misled. There is a problem, and it is not just with students. It appears to be with their parents as well.

So although the homecoming was somewhat improved, it wasn't all it could or should have been. The principal had gone on the public address system the week before to downplay the rules. He didn't enforce the contract by removing two-time offenders from the dance, as other principals had the previous spring.

Still, though people had said nothing would come of his efforts, Christian had accomplished the beginning of something good that eventually spread beyond our county as the neighboring county recently adopted a similar contract for school dances. Through it all, Christian remained calm, poised, and ready to discuss his position with anyone who asked—from belligerent peers to journalists and television reporters. By the time this book is out, he'll be in a prestigious college, with a dual major in political science and music composition.

I caught up with Christian shortly before graduation to get the scoop on how this all played out for him personally.

Question: Please tell me about the reaction of your peers at school and teachers.

"There were very mixed reactions, though the most noticeable were the negative. It wasn't uncommon to hear curse words muttered in my direction as I walked down the hall. Most of my teachers were indifferent, but my psychology teacher actually tried to get my classmates worked up over the issue. He got a real kick out of it. He wasn't being antagonistic towards me (in fact, I think he shared my viewpoint)—he just liked to get everyone riled up.

"There was one teacher who was especially hostile. Because of her heavy involvement with the prom, I believe she was personally offended by my attempt to influence the music and type of dancing at our school dances. Sadly, she didn't handle her frustration in an appropriate manner. Instead of speaking with me personally, she ranted to her classes for several days about me, my arrogance, my insolence, my rudeness, and my lack of respect for the school. She used her position of leadership as a platform for slander. When her students informed me of what she was doing in class, I was especially disappointed, because I expected more reasonable behavior from adults.

"One of the reactions that I had not anticipated was from several members of the school board and school administration: denial. Our school takes pride in being one of the best public schools in the country. We have high test scores and relatively few problems with vandalism, violence, drugs, gangs, and so on. Accordingly, they simply refused to believe that the honorable students of Loudoun Valley could be doing anything wrong. Many adults were more worried about the reputation of our school than about correcting the problem. In truth, this dancing takes place at almost every high school in the country. It just so happens that our school has students who aren't content with mediocrity.

"Most students were actually afraid to talk to me. They knew that I would not let myself be belittled and that I was quite capable at expressing my opinion. Most of the students who wanted to express their disagreement did so in base and vulgar ways, not actually addressing the issues. I can count on one hand the number of students who respectfully came to me, wanted to know what happened, what I believed, why I was speaking out, and then expressed their own thoughts. I greatly respect and appreciate those students.

"I also appreciate those students who privately gave me encouragement. Many were afraid to express their position in front of their peers for fear of being ridiculed."

I think God loves it when we stand up for what's right, because in doing so we must rely completely on Him. Listen to Christian's responses to these questions.

# Get Involved!

Fear of ridicule can be paralyzing, but standing up for faith and values is too important to be governed by fear. The Kansas City focus group teens had some valuable ideas of how parents can help their teens stand strong. Since we received them after our transcriber left, these comments are from handwritten notes, and some are not attributed. Still, great advice:

Matt: "There was a group of guys I was friends with in elementary school. As I got in high school, they started drinking and stuff. I kept refusing when they offered me drinks. Then another guy who really didn't want to drink had the courage to say no."

Michael: "You may be ridiculed for your faith, but they respect you. Sometimes they laugh at 'church boy,' then come up later and say, "I'm sorry. I didn't mean it."

Matt: "If you take a stand, you'll be persecuted. Your example is the best way to take a stand without having to say anything, and your example is directly related to the example your parents have set for you."

- Other people may tease and ridicule you for taking a stand, but that doesn't mean they don't respect you. Parents need to remind kids of this from time to time.

- Little encouragements are important. Remember to support your kids and remind them that what they're doing will impact others. Giving them Bible verses to help and praying with them means a lot—even if it doesn't seem like it at the time.

- Let your kids know that they'll be persecuted at some point. Prepare them for it, and when it happens, endure and encourage them through it, but don't try to keep them from it. The lessons they'll learn are important.

Were you ever afraid?

"Not really."

What sustained you—what are your favorite Bible verses?

"Col. 3:23-24—'Whatever you do, work at it with all your heart, as working for the Lord, not for men, since you know that you will receive an inheritance from the Lord as a reward. It is the Lord Christ you are serving.'

"At a time when most kids are paralyzingly worried about what their peers think of them, this is an awesome reminder that our validation is found in Christ."

What do you think made you the way you are?

"The assurance that I have been saved by grace through Jesus Christ has definitely affected the way I live. And as far as talents are concerned, credit goes to God—I just have to remember to develop my skills."

Was it hard for you to go through what you went through?

"Not really. I'm a pretty relaxed individual, and I was frankly surprised at how worked-up the community got. And considering the persecution faced by Christians in other nations, I believe it would be a shame to claim any real hardship."

Christian obviously has a calling for leadership, and what he went through was a big deal because it was very public. But every Christian kid faces his or her own challenges while trying to live as salt and light in the world. Make sure your kids have the opportunity to tell you what's going on so you can love and encourage them through it.

Even as I put the finishing touches on this chapter, I received the following new message from Kristen, who gave up an acting opportunity, mentioned earlier in this chapter. This time there was a happier ending:

After an audition, I was selected to be part of a 10-minute play in a festival at my university. The script itself was not bad, although my character cursed once. My director, however, decided to manipulate a few lines to make them very vulgar with accompanying gestures and such, and I was becoming more convicted to not be in this play. (My personal test is "Does this bring glory to God?") At any rate, I decided that it would be necessary for me to resign. I spoke with my director about it, but he told me that he did not want me to go because he couldn't imagine anyone else doing such a great job with the part. So he changed everything I had a problem with! It was pretty incredible. It's nice to know that you can stand up for your beliefs and still be involved in activities you love.

Bottom Line for Parents

- Ask your teen about pressures or problems at school—and at youth group.
- Ask your teen how you can pray for him or her, and then do it.
- Let your teen make some moral choices on his or her own.
- Encourage and equip your teen with relevant Bible verses.
- If a problem seems too big for your teen to handle, ask if he or she wants help.
- Set an example—stand up for what's right.

6. MAKING THE MOST OF MISTAKES

Self-help

"My kids will never act like that!"

Remember those proud promises you used to make—scoffing at the inferior job other parents were doing when you saw kids in full tantrum mode at Wal-Mart? Or even whining just a little for a treat? Yes, once upon a time we were all parenting experts—and weren't those the days? Back before we had kids of our own.

But once our little miracles hit a certain age, they become vivid reminders that, yes, indeed, "All have sinned and fall short of the glory of God." And if we're completely honest about our own parenting, we know we have too.

In the beginning of the book I mentioned that my parenting before I became a Christian left a lot to be desired. I would like to go back and fill in the background. I think it will help you see why I encourage parents never to write anyone off—no matter how far he or she has strayed—and why I believe it's important for every parent to

- accept that your children—and you as well—will make mistakes;
- learn to make the most of each one.

Let me give you my life in a nutshell: By the time I was five, I had lived in six different towns—from Atlanta to Fairbanks, Alaska, to Long Beach, California. My father was a drifter who ran up bills in one place, then moved on to the next. He abandoned my mother, my two younger brothers, and me when I was six. My mother put us in an unofficial foster home where we were abused. When we came home to live, we never saw much of her. She worked two or three jobs to support us, and her spare time was consumed by problems with alcohol and problems with men. We didn't have enough money for a car and sometimes did not have enough to eat. That would have been OK if two other things had not been lacking as well: love and faith.

I didn't know what was missing, but I knew I wanted a better life, so I worked hard at my education, even becoming a National Merit Scholar. I married a kind and loving man, who put me through college and Montessori teacher training. We had two daughters: Samantha Sunshine and Jasmine Moondance. Yes, we were hippies. And so even as there were positive things going on in my life, there were the negatives too: drugs, promiscuity, and radical politics.

Eventually, though I had educated myself, I ended up much like my mother—divorced (though I was the one who abandoned someone who didn't deserve it) and drowning in problems with drugs, alcohol, and men.

In 1980, for the first time I called out to God for help. With no church background and living in a very anti-Christian county in California, I never thought of going to church. Instead, I sought help through Alcoholics Anonymous, where I learned to live a life without drugs and alcohol one day at a time. I was also introduced to the concept of a "higher power," which set me looking for God, but in all the wrong places, like New Age, prosperity thinking, and meditation. In 1983 I met a man who was also a sincere spiritual seeker. When I became pregnant three months later, Tripp and I immediately married and then began building a business and having a slue of children together—even as we continued our spiritual journey. In 1987, seemingly quite by accident, we became Christians. And our lives were never the same.

OK—you may be wondering how that résumé positions me to be any kind of authority on parenting. With solid-rock Christians filling bookstore shelves with rock-solid advice, what of any value does someone like me, who's known God for only 17 years, little more than one third of her life, have to communicate?

Believe me—I've asked myself those questions. But I find assurance in the words Paul wrote in 1 Tim. 1:15-16: "Here is a trustworthy saying that deserves full acceptance: Christ Jesus came into the world to save sinners—of whom I am the worst. But for that very reason I was shown mercy so that in me, the worst of sinners, Christ Jesus might display his unlimited patience as an example for those who would believe on him and receive eternal life."

I never doubted that God loved me as much as He loved all the other believers who had never sinned so grievously against Him. He had left plenty of clues that He was always there, waiting for us to turn around and start heading in the right direction.

There were the circumstances of Tripp's and my salvation, which obviously only *seemed* accidental. As counterculture, political leftists, we had only scorn for Christianity and chose Eastern religion from the New Age buffet of beliefs. However, no matter how successful we were at finding harmony in the universe, we

What Does God Say?

If anyone is in Christ, he is a new creation; the old has gone, the new has come (2 Cor. 5:17).

As far as the east is from the west, so far has he removed our transgressions from us (Ps. 103:12).

could not find it in our home. Since we each believed in our own divinity, we were selfish, stubborn, and full of pride.

In 1987 I was ready to give up on my second marriage when I heard Dennis and Barbara Rainey on James Dobson's *Focus on the Family* radio show (I used to listen to him for parenting advice but turned off the Christian station in disgust when someone I judged to be a "Bible-thumper," like Warren Wiersbe, came on). The Raineys were talking about a conference coming up that weekend in San Francisco. In desperation, I signed us up. Tripp and I fought all the way down on Friday night. Our situation certainly seemed hopeless.

What we didn't know was that on Saturday morning our lives would be irrevocably changed. That was the day we first heard the Good News simply presented with Campus Crusade for Christ's "Four Spiritual Laws":

1. God loves you and has a wonderful plan for your life.
2. We are separated from God by sin.
3. Jesus is the only provision to have relationship with God.
4. Each individual must make a decision to receive Jesus to experience God's plan.

Though Tripp and I had known about Jesus, we had thought of Him simply as a great spiritual teacher. We had His picture on our meditation table along with those of all the other gurus whose wisdom we tried to follow. This was the first time we had heard the truth about who He was. We did receive Jesus, then and there, on March 21, 1987. Tears were streaming down our faces, and we knew something profound had happened. It wasn't until we came home and started reading the Bible that we found the verse that diagnosed our condition: we had been born again! Now we were like all those people we never wanted to be like.

I guess what we never understood was that all those people we never wanted to be like were followers of Christ. We had become not followers of Christians but followers of Christ. And I know we were being obedient to the Holy Spirit as we made decisions—like throwing away our New Age library—before we ever went to church and had someone tell us the right thing to do.

Still, it was quite a comedown from our self-image as highly evolved spiritual beings to new followers of Christ who didn't even know the New Testament from the Old. And we both felt a sense of urgency to hurry up and get this parenting thing right. As we looked back over both sides of the family tree, we found it full of divorce, alcoholism, and homosexuality. We felt God had positioned us to be a turning point in our family legacy. And we understood He had been guiding us all along. Something supernatural had certainly intervened when I learned I was pregnant and we were nudged away from an abortion and into marriage. Then God left His fingerprints all over the first four years of our marriage by the names we (He) had chosen for our sons: Joshua Gabriel, Matthew Raphael, and Benjamin Michael.

In addition to the sense of urgency about becoming good Christian parents, there was also extreme gratitude to God for giving us a second chance. And finally, there was something particularly unique, part of the experience of coming to know Christ later in life: everything I thought I knew was now up for grabs. When my beliefs turned 180 degrees as the light of truth illuminated each area, there was little I took for granted, few "certainties" I would hold to from the past. I was almost like a blank slate when it came to parenting, offering myself to God as a mother: *Write your will for me as a parent on my heart, Lord. Teach me how to do this to your glory.*

I couldn't have been more sincere. I not only wanted—and was willing to work—to be the best parent I could be, but I had a long-range vision of raising my children to be the best parents they could be as well. Years before Rick Warren wrote "Purpose-Driven" anything, I was practicing purpose-driven parenting!

Today Tripp and I have 12 children. The two oldest girls

 Get Involved!

Consider Jonathan Edwards, the great American theologian, who with his wife, Sarah, raised 11 children.

In 1925 Princeton scholar Benjamin B. Warfield charted Edwards' 1,394 known descendants. They included 13 college presidents, 65 college professors, 30 judges, 100 lawyers, 60 physicians, 75 military officers, 100 pastors, 60 authors, 3 United States senators, 80 public servants in other capacities including governors and ministers to foreign countries, and one vice-president of the United States.

Following are the conclusions drawn by Family First (<www .familyfirst.net>):

"The story of Jonathan Edwards is an example of what some sociologists call the 'five-generation rule.' How parents raise their child—the love they give, the values they teach, the emotional environment they offer, the education they provide— influences not only their child but the four generations to follow. What [parents] do, in other words, will reach through the next five generations. The example of Jonathan Edwards shows just how rich that legacy can be.

"But the five-generation rule works both ways. If we fail to work at being good [parents], our neglect can plague generations. Consider the case of Max Jukes, a contemporary of Edwards. As an adult, Jukes had a drinking problem that kept him from holding a steady job. It also kept him from showing much concern for his wife and children. He would disappear sometimes for days and return drunk. He made little time for loving and instructing his children.

"Benjamin Warfield has also charted Jukes' descendants. What he found further supports the five-generation rule. Warfield was able to trace 540 of Jukes' ancestors.

"They offer a stunning contrast to the Edwards' legacy. Of Jukes' known descendents, 310 died as paupers, at least 150 were criminals (including 7 murderers), more than 100 were drunkards, and half of his female descendents ended up as prostitutes."

While there is some dispute as to the exact numbers of

Jukes' descendants, even those who claim some turned out OK note that none rose above the level of farmer or artisan. While there's nothing dishonorable about those callings, the high calling of the Edwards' family still stands out as an example of what can happen when we bring a strong sense of purpose to parenthood.

are grown up with Christian families of their own—Samantha and Kip have five, Jasmine and Nathan have four. My boys are Josh, 21 (getting married soon), Matt, 20 (on his own—see the end of this chapter), Ben, 18 (studying voice at Liberty University), and Zach, 17 (headed for college at this writing). Sophia and Madeleine are 15 and 12. Jonny, who has Down syndrome, is 13. And our three adopted sons with Down syndrome are Jesse, 9, Daniel, 8, and Justin, 5.

All this is to say that God—through giving me 35 years of raising children, 17 years of following him, and 10 years of developing my communication skills—has enabled me to earn a unique spot on the parenting shelf. My perspective may be just a little more real because nothing's really theoretical with me. I've been through it all, and I'm still going through it.

For one thing, I'm still staying up waiting for teens to come home at night and then getting up early the next morning with toddlers; still driving to Little League and play practice; still being reminded daily that no matter how hard I try, I'll never be the perfect parent.

Think about it: 12 kids and 35 years of parenting give a mom a sky-high exposure rate. Compared to someone with three kids, I'm four times more likely on any given day to have something go wrong (because even my grown kids can have something go wrong). If there were mommy insurance, no one would underwrite mine—too risky.

The upside is all the experience I've had helping my kids learn to make the most of their mistakes. You can trust that this chapter is one that's dear to my heart and very, very real. I believe that learning to make the most of mistakes is one of the greatest gifts we can give our kids.

Here's how the process started for me:

It was when I cried out to God to help me get over my dependence on alcohol and drugs that I learned to admit my mistakes. It was in Alcoholics Anonymous (AA) that I learned to be brutally honest with myself and others about my mistakes. And it was through the 12 Steps of AA that I learned how to make the most of them.

Even before I became a believer, I had learned to search my conscience for the ways I had harmed others (they don't call it sin in AA, but that's what it is), and I had learned to apologize. I had "made amends" to those I had hurt—most importantly, my ex-husband and my daughters.

When I apologized to my daughters, I was very specific about the things I had done wrong, no holds barred and no excuses. I had neglected Samantha and Jasmine, I had given them too much responsibility at too young an age, and I had put them in harm's way.

I never considered my initial apology to be the end of the matter but the opening of a lifetime conversation. It had hurt me so much that my own mother refused to discuss the past with me. I told my girls that they could bring up anything they needed anytime, and I would apologize again. Over the years we have spoken with regret over their less-than-ideal early years. And while the words "I'm sorry" can't take away the past, speaking and hearing them are like a healing balm. Samantha and Jasmine and I have a closeness we couldn't possibly have if I had insisted on burying the past.

Do you see where I'm coming from in this chapter? Before we can begin to teach our children how to make the most of their mistakes, we must find the humility to deal with our own and the willingness to let God help us make the most of them.

I was fortunate in that I had learned to do these things before I became a believer, for as I said, Tripp and I already had responsibility for five children, so our training as Christian parents would be on-the-job. I needed all the help I could get.

Discussion Starters

Parents with less-than-desirable pasts are often hesitant to own up to the mistakes they made when they were young, worried their kids will get the message that it's OK to stray as long as you get back to the flock later on. But listen to these poignant comments:

- "Actually, my parents rarely admit or inform us of their mistakes, and when they do, it's tiny stuff, like, my mom said she 'dated too many guys.' I wish they would admit more, because it shows that they've gone through the same things we might be going through and that they know from experience what's best and can help us with our hard times. It also would make us want to talk to them more about our private lives and hear more of their advice. That would prevent a whole lot of kids from making big mistakes. At least that's how I feel."

- "It's really important that parents talk to their kids about the mistakes they made and why it was bad for them, not just the generic 'Oh, you shouldn't do that—it's bad for you' conversation. My dad told me that he used to smoke a lot, and he made sure I knew better than to take that up. But there are some things my parents haven't talked to me about that I wish they had. My mom said something to me one time, and I found out that my dad had smoked marijuana when he was a teenager, but he would never tell me that himself. I've also always wondered if my parents were virgins when they got married, but I'm too embarrassed to ask. *I want to know more about their lives and how they struggled when they were teens, because I think it would have helped me to hear my parents' personal stories about some of the trials I face. I wish my parents had talked with me more about those types of things, even though they assumed I would never be involved in drugs or anything*" (emphasis added).

With no Christian background, Tripp and I did not understand what had happened to us until three weeks later we read the Bible verse about being born again. Then it took another week or so to understand the ramifications of the rebirth in terms of needing to go to church. We had no mentors, only the Bible and God—Father, Son, and Holy Spirit—to rely on. But hey—that's a lot, especially for parents who had never had that kind of help.

It was help we could have used the year before, when Samantha decided to move in with her dad. With no spiritual grounding, she and I had come to an impasse in our conflicted relationship. She had also announced she was sick of my having babies every 18 months.

Now, suddenly, a year later she wanted to come home.

"Why?" I asked. "After all, the only thing that's changed is that we have another baby."

Still, she insisted and began moving her stuff back home, one carload at a time. We were living in a little fairy tale house next to a creek at the end of a road. I say fairy tale, because the house had been made from a barn into a two-story home, and the ceilings upstairs were so low that Tripp had to bend his head a little when he was up there. The house had a little cottage with two bedrooms, and since all the bedrooms inside were needed for little kids, Samantha would be staying in the cottage. I was going over the rules with her one sunshiny morning as she helped me make my bed: "And, of course, when Kip comes, he won't be allowed to visit you in the cottage. You two will need to hang out in the main house."

Suddenly the sheet Samantha and I had been flapping went slack.

"What are you talking about?" she demanded. Of course, it was understandable that she might balk at rules when I had been raising her for so long without them. Even I could hardly understand these new ideas coming out of my mouth as though someone else had taken over for me.

"Don't you trust us?" she asked, accusingly.

"Well, of course, I trust you, Honey, but greater people than you have given into temptation," I replied. And it was true. I did trust her, even though I had no reason to, since I hadn't brought her up with any moral compass, and all this talk was new to us.

"Well, for your information, we already *do* it," Samantha spat out, as though those words would be my ultimate defeat.

I dropped my corners of the sheet, walked over, and put my arms around her.

"Well, Honey, I forgive you, and so does Jesus." *Where in the world were these words coming from?* This was all so new to me. As a former sexual revolutionary, I had never taught my daughter that premarital sex was wrong or something you needed to be forgiven for.

But somewhere deep inside, Samantha knew. And those words just melted the hardness of her heart. She was sobbing, "I know somehow it's wrong, and we try to stop, but after a few weeks we just can't help it."

"That's because you don't have God in your life," I said. *Where did* that *come from?*

Samantha knew she had made a mistake and was prepared to deal with it. But how would Kip handle it? Tripp called him and asked him to meet him at his office the next day, which happened to be Father's Day. Samantha somehow avoided talking to him, so Kip went in cold.

It was a man–to–man talk, so I don't know all the details. I assume Tripp was led as blindly as I through all the things God wanted said. Tripp showed Kip the appropriate Bible verses, the thou–shalt–nots. But he also gave him a positive, practical application:

"Do you love Samantha?" he asked.

"Yes," Kip said.

"Well, she's never going to know for sure unless you can

take sex out of the equation of your relationship until the right time," Tripp said.

Now it may seem ironic that two people whose lives had been filled with so much sexual sin could speak with any authority about purity to these two teenagers. And maybe if we had been Christians longer, we would have thought too much about it and lost our steam. But we were newly saved and so humble, therefore so dependent on God to handle each new situation that presented itself. We could not have explained it then, but looking back, I just see us standing in confidence on the fact that God loved us and had forgiven us and that as new creations in Christ, we could speak the truth without being ashamed that we hadn't known it ourselves.

Samantha and Kip's story has a very happy ending. Not only did they commit their lives to God, but they committed their relationship as well. They conducted the rest of their relationship on a different footing, more under parental oversight—as it should have been from the beginning. They reestablished their purity and maintained it.

When sex is introduced into an unmarried relationship, it often takes on a life of its own—crowding out all the other ways in which a man and woman develop closeness and learn about each other. Samantha remembers the next two years of their relationship—with the pressure of sex removed—as being extremely rewarding.

When Kip asked Tripp if he could marry Samantha, even though they were only 19, we knew they had proven themselves to be mature and ready. After their marriage, they both worked while Kip finished college. Now, 15 years later, they have a strong, committed marriage and five children.

Do Kip and Samantha wish they had never made a mistake in the first place? I'm sure they do. But they use their experience to help others turn toward God rather than away from Him. This weekend they'll be speaking at a youth group on how teens who have lost their virginity can submit their lives to

God to restore their purity. They learned at a very young age that when our lives are submitted to God, He can use anything to His glory.

They made the most of a big mistake.

How had the teens I interviewed dealt with mistakes? Those who shared specifics with me were unanimous in asking that their names not be mentioned:

Question: Have you ever blown it completely?

"Yes, I have. A friend of mine introduced me to a friend she had met the previous year. We started talking over the Internet, and before we knew it, he had asked me to be his girlfriend, and we had established a long-distance relationship. My first mistake, looking back, was agreeing to a long-distance relationship —especially with someone I hadn't even met. Things went well for a while, but we started to talk about things we shouldn't have, and things quickly went downhill from there. Pretty soon our relationship had shifted from talking about God and what we were learning to talking about physical things. He broke up with me after a month, and I thought it was the most horrible thing that ever happened to me."

How did God use it for good?

"God taught me so many things! He taught me that I must absolutely not lower my standards of physical purity. And thankfully, He taught me in a context where I couldn't actually do anything that we were talking about. He taught me a very valuable lesson while protecting my physical body. He also taught me that I need to rely on Him more than a boyfriend and desire Him more than a boyfriend. God needs to be number one in my life! He also taught me how to forgive probably more than I ever have before."

Question: Have you ever blown it completely? How did you learn from it? Who helped you, and how?

"I've messed up so much it isn't even funny. For instance, once I cheated on math for an entire school year (I'm homeschooled) and had to make it all up the next year (double work all year)—not to mention that my parents weren't exactly thrilled with me. My brother helped me through it by tutoring me. I learned that even when the going gets tough (I cheated to save face because I didn't understand it), not to give in to the easy way.

Question: Have you ever blown it completely or almost completely? What happened? How did you learn from it? Who helped you and how?

"I blew it completely (so it seemed at the time). I was driving 35 in a 25 with my mom in the car, and right after she told me to slow down, I got a ticket. I was crying and very upset, as I knew it would mean higher insurance rates and most likely a lecture about driving. I learned it was probably for the better, because a wreck would have been much more expensive than one ticket."

How did God use it for good?

"God used it for good by helping me see that my mom isn't always wrong and that maybe I should listen to her more often."

Question: Have you ever blown it completely? How did you learn from it? Who helped you, and how?

"I was in the eighth grade and had a test the next morning I hadn't studied for. My parents and I were at each other's throats that night about my neglecting my chores around the house. I was frustrated because I couldn't organize my thoughts to defend myself, plus the pressure of a test I was unprepared for. I ran upstairs, packed a small bag of clothes and food, and ran out of the house before my parents could react. I assume they thought I had gone out for a short walk to clear my mind; instead, I was headed down a dark two-lane highway with thoughts exploding in my head. Seven miles later, I stopped at a run-down barn, spread out some hay in a corner, and plopped down to rest.

"I woke up several hours later, the moon overhead, scared. It finally hit me: I was running away from my problems. And then it occurred to me—what type of person does this make me? How was running away going to solve any of my problems? At this moment, I knew what I had to do. Somehow I gathered my courage and knocked on the door of the farm house, asked if I could use the phone, and called my dad.

"At home I was immediately sent to my room. I flopped on the bed and just bawled my eyes out. Sometime later, my parents, both of them, came into my room and sat on the bed comforting me, which made me cry even more. When I finally got my breath back, I started talking. I must have talked for an hour straight, pouring out my soul, saying everything I had wanted to say several hours earlier. They did the best thing a parent can do for a teenager: they listened. They didn't interrupt, make disappointed faces, or push for more on a subject that interested them. When I ran out of things to say, we were all crying our eyes out. We spent the better part of the night talking and crying, talking and crying, and talking some more, which helped us understand where this was coming from and how to avoid such arguments in the future."

Question: Have you ever blown it completely? What happened? How did you learn from it? Who helped you, and how?

"I blew it—completely. I took the first step into the false, dark world of pornography. Curiosity was warped into lust at the too-young age of 14, but any age is the wrong one for porn. I was involved in that dark online cycle for quite a few months when finally my mom asked me one day in the car how I was doing, and I caved. There are always those stories about the weight being lifted from one's shoulders once confession happens, and I didn't realize how true those stories are until my secret was exposed into the light. My mom's routine question about how I was doing was what helped me come back to full repentance. Once we got home, we talked with my dad, and by the end of the night, I had two allies with me in the trenches against this temptation."

How did God use it for good?

"Today, at the age of 17, I know the threat for what it really is. I know that the temptation and the threat are always there. I don't say that I'm recovered but that I now recognize the temptation for what it really is and cling to God all the more because of it. I now know where and when I'm most tempted and can take measures to avoid falling to temptation again. I know my own weaknesses, and more and more readily I cling to God for guidance."

These stories of mistakes, while differing in gravity, all have one thing in common: they've been resolved. These teens took the necessary steps. They admitted they made a mistake. They decided to change. They sought God's help, and sometimes their parents' help.

Discussion Starters

Be sensitive to signs that your teen might be wrestling with a problem. Don't expect it to come out with just a simple "Is something wrong?" Instead, try to prepare some special one-on-one time, and pray that God will help it to be revealed.

Teens told me that when they failed to meet their parents' expectations, they desperately needed to know their parents still loved them:

Michael, a senior at a Christian high school and part of the Kansas City focus group: "I think if your parents yell at you or lecture you, you're not going to say anything to them. But if they're going to accept you with love and help you fix your problem instead of coming down on you for it, then it's going to be a lot easier to talk to them and have that trust. And if you have that trust, it's a lot easier to deal with the problem."

Rick: "It's a lot easier for the kids to talk if the parents aren't going to blow up and scream and yell. I think parents still need to discipline but also need to show love. You know—'You messed up, but we still love you.'"

What happens when a teen chooses the wrong path and refuses to admit it or do anything to change?

Unfortunately, we've had this experience in our family.

When we moved to Virginia, my second son was anxious to get a girlfriend. The first girl he liked was modest, pretty, and much too serious a student to be interested in a laid-back guy like Matt. The next girl was clearly not on the same page values-wise. Matt had taken a wait-until-marriage vow, so when he tried to avoid kissing, her reaction was to break up with him and spread rumors that he was gay.

Matt's next girlfriend was from a large Christian family, and, assuming her family embraced the same values, we breathed a sigh of relief. We just didn't see what was coming.

There was a combination of forces at work: Matt's earlier involvement with pornography and the chip on his shoulder because of the rumors he was gay. Matt went from first kiss to sex in about a month.

How did we know? The girl told Matt's younger brother, violating his innocence too. In the meantime, Matt had developed a pattern of lying. Ironically, he was always the son who was sure to call anytime he changed location. I didn't realize until later that it was all a cover-up.

When we told Matt he couldn't see her anymore, he begged, pleaded, promised, and became irrational, saying they "were married in God's eyes." We tried to explain that the intense bond he felt was understandable because that was the bond God wanted for marriage. Our words fell on seemingly deaf ears. (We found out later that she had another more serious boyfriend all along.) Her parents would not cooperate, sheltering him and playing the role of understanding parents in a "good parents, bad parents" game.

The situation could not continue, as there were eight children younger than Matt at home. Their futures would be impacted by how we handled this. We planned an intervention— based on the model used with addicts—surprising Matt one

Get Involved!

What happens when Christian teenagers become parents? While perhaps in the past there was too much judgment and shame, I would like to suggest that the pendulum toward mercy and grace may have swung too far to the other side.

At one church, the Christmas pageant director gave the part of Mary to a pregnant 16-year-old. When asked why he passed over a dozen girls who had maintained their purity, he said he wanted to show mercy and forgiveness.

Of course, we do want to show mercy and forgiveness to young people who have made wrong choices, and it's important to make sure the baby's needs are met. But we must be careful to not give all our attention to these situations while the teens who are struggling to live their lives according to God's laws receive minimal encouragement or recognition.

day when he came home from work with a living room full of people who loved him: youth pastor, married sisters and brothers-in-law, brothers and sisters, Mom and Dad, and his two best Christian buddies and accountability partners.

For three hours we spoke the truth with love to Matt. His dad brought out the journal they kept when they went away for their Growing into Manhood weekend and read the entries they had made. Each person there had a special insight or memory or piece of encouragement for Matt to turn away from the sin in his life and come back to the people and the God who loved him. Listening, I felt proud of my kids and their friends for their capacity for caring. All of us cried. All of our hearts were breaking.

The bottom line was that Matt had to make a decision. He was 18 years old. We were still responsible for him and his education. He wanted to be an actor, so that meant that he needed college. He could place himself back under our authority and stop seeing the girl, or he could move out and begin his own life.

If he moved out, we would give him $500 and the title to the car we let him drive, but that would be the end of our responsibility.

It was extremely difficult, but after a few hours and then some one-on-one with his youth pastor, Matt finally broke. "Can I use the phone for 15 minutes to call her to break up?" he asked.

"Sure," I said and started checking my watch.

I didn't need to. Before the 15 minutes was up, Matt was loading his stuff into boxes and into his car.

Our family was devastated, of course. It was the greatest heartbreak Tripp and I could have imagined as Christian parents, to see our child make the wrong choice, to hear him say the wrong good-bye. And though I joked about it at the beginning of this chapter, it's really no joke that every conscientious parent feels that things like this will never happen to him or her. It helped that I had some high-profile Christian friends who had been through the same thing. I knew of prodigals who had come back, like Franklin Graham. Some parents were still waiting.

I cried for three weeks solid, barely able to do the laundry. It was hard to explain the profound depths of my grief—almost as though a child had died—well, a child *had* died, spiritually.

Though initially Tripp and I felt great shame in having a child turn away from the Lord—and as a "parenting expert" I felt a double burden—more mature Christians reminded us that God gives each of us free will and that no matter how hard we work to bring up our children in "the fear and admonition of the Lord," we can't control the results.

"After all," one friend said, "God's first children, whose life in the Garden of Eden was perfect, turned from Him."

The important thing for us to know was that we did everything we could to get Matt back on track, that we clearly communicated our love, but finally Matt had to deal with the consequences of his decision.

Ironically, the girl Matt gave up everything for dumped him a month later. But Matt, enjoying his newfound "freedom," got

What Does God Say?

Train a child in the way he should go, and when he is old he will not turn from it (Prov. 22:6).

I will pour water on the thirsty land, and streams on the dry ground; I will pour out my Spirit on your offspring, and my blessing on your descendants. They will spring up like grass in a meadow, like poplar trees by flowing streams (Isa. 44:3-4).

a job in a dinner theater and a place to live about 90 minutes from home. He stopped going to church or seeking out believers. Though he managed to support himself—and we were proud of him for that—we grieved that he had given himself over to a life apart from God.

Some in the Christian community thought we should disavow Matt as our son. But that just doesn't sound like the father of the prodigal Jesus told us of. Although it wasn't comfortable or easy at first, we welcomed Matt on holidays and any other times he wanted to show up—which came to only three or four times a year. Someday, I'm sure, we'll welcome him back into the family of God.

In the meantime, Matt's turning-away from God has already been used for good in the lives of others, particularly his brothers and friends, whose faith and commitment to personal purity was strengthened by seeing the toll sin takes on an individual's life as well as those who love him.

Our family's favorite hymn is "Come, Thou Fount of Every Blessing" (for tune and lyrics of this and approximately 4,500 other hymns, go to <www.cyberhymnal.org>). My favorite verse is the second:

Here I raise my Ebenezer;
Hither by Thy help I've come.
And I hope, by Thy good pleasure,
Safely to arrive at home.
Jesus sought me when a stranger,
Wand'ring from the fold of God
He, to rescue me from danger,
Interposed His precious blood.

—Robert Robinson

"Ebenezer," which means "stone of help," comes from 1 Sam. 7:12, when the Israelites cried out to God and were saved from the Philistines: "Then Samuel took a stone and set it up between Mizpah and Shen. He named it Ebenezer, saying, 'Thus far has the LORD helped us.'"

We have those dramatic moments in our lives too, as individuals and as families—times when things could have gone one way but God turned them around for good. Sometimes those moments are based on mistakes we've made, mistakes that the enemy would like to use to silence and shame us.

I say, "Turn the tables." Raise your Ebenezers, and teach your kids to raise their own wherever there's been a spiritual turning point in their lives. Take mistakes out of the enemy's arsenal, and let God use them for good to make them stronger.

I mentioned earlier that I was pregnant when Tripp married me. After becoming Christians, rather than feeling ashamed and hiding that from our kids, we raised it as an Ebenezer. The fact was, Tripp and I did not have the character to make the right decision. We know that God—though we didn't yet know Him—must have intervened to move us to choose to have the baby and to get married, moving us that much farther along in His plan for our lives.

The fact is, if there hadn't been Joshua, there probably wouldn't have been the rest of the Curtis family. Each year before we light the candles for his birthday, we tell the story of how God used Joshua to nudge us into a commitment we might not have otherwise made. Josh is the cornerstone on which God began to build and continues to build a strong Christian family.

As Zan Tyler has written, "God doesn't have to have a lot to work with in order to do great things in our lives, or in the lives of our children." Learning to make the most of our mistakes just speeds up the process.

Bottom Line for Parents

- Accept the fact that your children—and you as parents—will make mistakes.
- Teach your children to admit mistakes quickly.
- Make it safe for your kids to confide their mistakes in you.
- Help them see mistakes as learning opportunities.
- Pray with them for God's help.
- Use tough love when necessary.
- Give thanks for the Ebenezers—spiritual turnarounds—in your family's history.

7. LIVING WITH INTEGRITY

Self-satisfaction

When my oldest son, Josh, was a freshman in college, his literature class was assigned to read *The Awakening*, a "rediscovered" 1899 novel favored by feminist professors. The book tells the story of a pampered woman who grows dissatisfied with her traditional life—husband and children—and escapes to pursue her freedom. She finds freedom in painting, gambling, affairs, and in the end committing suicide.

Since this book is pretty common freshman fare, there are more than 300 reviews at <www.amazon.com>. Here's a typical one:

> *The Awakening* is a compelling portrait of a woman discovering her own identity and demanding to be treated as an autonomous human being, consequently rebelling against the norms of society. . . . This novella will remind readers of Gustave Flaubert's *Madame Bovary*, but the differences are significant and reflect more than the fact one was written by a Frenchman and the other by an American woman. *The Awakening* is more sensual and its heroine eminently more worthy of sympathy and admiration.

Nowadays it's certainly not rare for a woman to leave her family to pursue her own desires. But since in 1899 this would have been so unheard of, *The Awakening* is seen by those of a certain mind-set to be some sort of masterpiece. And the discussion that went on in Josh's class was probably pretty much the same that goes on in freshman literature classes throughout our free-thinking universities: heaps of praise for the heroine, who had been able to transcend the "stifling" social code of her era, and great admiration for the author, whose vision could encompass the as-yet-unrealized liberation of women from the shackles of matrimony and childrearing.

Josh was left completely puzzled.

"Mom, I don't get it," he said after reading the book. "If this were a story about a man who left his wife and kids to find his freedom, we wouldn't think of him as a hero, would we?"

Right. And anyone who sends teens to college today needs to know they're exposing their kids to tremendous risk, not on-

# Get Involved!

Two books I recommend for parents sending kids to college:

How to Stay Christian in College: An Interactive Guide to Keeping the Faith, by J. Budziszewski

This unique and reader-friendly book by a Christian college professor will help your student maintain his or her integrity under the slings and arrows of modern campus life. Give this to your teen, and read it yourself.

I Am Charlotte Simmons, by Tom Wolfe

President George W. Bush's recommendation of this book to friends made the news big-time in 2005, probably because a lot of off-color material is included in this fictional portrait of a poor, Christian, back-country girl with brains who wins a scholarship to a major Ivy League-type university. But it was undoubtedly the social commentary that was of most interest to the president. The tale of how the integrity of an innocent girl comes under attack and is eventually destroyed should be must reading for parents sending daughters to college. Recommended with extreme caution, as this modern-day *Pilgrim's Progress* is cluttered with lots of offensive content. Then again, so is college.

ly from corrupting curriculum and anti-Christian professors but also with the ridiculous freedom of coeducational dorms and bathrooms.

And while Christian colleges are definitely more protective, parents who think their kids will be completely safe there are just plain naive. I know because my son, Ben, goes to a Christian college, and he's shared a lot with me about the frailty, temptation, and sin within the student body.

That's not to say we should shun college, although I do think many more kids go to college than really should. But we need to be realistic about the challenges our kids will face and whether they're strong enough to maintain their integrity in an environment where it will be put to the test each day.

We must listen when our kids indicate God may have another plan than the one we had for their lives. While some parents have their minds made up from the get-go that all their kids will go to college, I've never agreed with that kind of thinking. It just doesn't leave much room for God to decide. And it's not realistic, because for some people, college is just not necessary. As the father says in the movie *Sorry, Wrong Number:* "If a man hasn't got a talent for making money, college won't knock it into him. And if a man has a talent for making money, he won't need college."

When Josh chose to leave college and get on with his life, his dad and I understood. He's always been a physical kind of guy, so it didn't surprise us when he decided to start a construction company with his brother-in-law Nathan. Now he's building his character through his work—which includes relating to many types of customers—even as he builds his company to support the family he and his fiancée, Hattie, hope to have someday.

I'm happy with how Josh turned out. He's the kind of man I wanted to raise. He's a leader, and he knows how to listen to women for the special wisdom they bring to the table. Having helped raise his younger brothers and sisters—and changed quite a few diapers in his lifetime—he's sure to be a capable and involved dad. At 21, he's grounded in God's love, sets his own limits, avoids temptation, displays compassion, has a track record of standing up for what's right, and has learned to make the most of his mistakes.

If those last six qualities sound familiar, they should, because they're the first six chapters of this book. Living with integrity involves all of those, plus a little extra.

Where does a parent find that little extra?

You're on your way when you see you need more than a blueprint for raising good kids. You need a vision. As I've brought several kids into adulthood while still teaching little ones to tie shoes, what has sustained me is feeling that God's purpose undergirds my parenthood. When I accepted God's purpose for my life at 38, I understood that though my life had never been without a purpose, I had never had a clue as to what it was. I didn't want my kids to grow up willy-nilly like that. I wanted them to trust in God and His purpose for their lives too.

Don't confuse having purpose with having goals. A child may want to grow up to be a doctor or an opera singer or a rocket scientist. Those are goals, not purposes. Goals are worldly ends we want to reach. Purpose is seen in how we get there.

What Does God Say?

If the LORD delights in a man's way, he makes his steps firm; though he stumble, he will not fall, for the LORD upholds him with his hand (Ps. 37:23-24).

The LORD God is a sun and shield; the LORD bestows favor and honor; no good thing does he withhold from those whose walk is blameless (Ps. 84:11).

Many parents, thinking long-range for their children, start college savings funds before the baby is sleeping through the night. But what's much more important than investing in our child's education is investing in his or her character. What kind of men and women do we want to produce? Knowing that has been extremely important to me in the responsibility I take for guiding my kids.

My kids have been educated in many settings: Christian school, homeschool, and public school. They've been to youth groups, Vacation Bible School, Sunday School, and Bible studies galore. But their dad and I are still the ones who oversee their daily lives, discuss with them the practical application of their spiritual knowledge, hold them accountable, and nudge them back on track when they're a little off. We know them better than anyone. That's our job as parents.

There's a word that describes what I've had in mind as I raised Josh and his brothers and sisters: *mensch*. It's one of those Yiddish words. Yiddish is a Germanic language written in Hebrew that includes many special Hebrew words, especially those that have to do with faith. It's a challenge to translate, but because it means exactly what I'm talking about here, I'll try.

The German language has the word *mann* for man. But *mensch* means so much more. One dictionary defines *mensch* as "a person having admirable characteristics, such as fortitude and firmness of purpose." *Mensch* also signifies a perfect gentleman or a perfect lady, someone compassionate, caring, and kind.

So when I think about the kind of adults I want my children to grow up to be, I'm thinking *menschen*—men and women with good, strong, and gracious character. I'm not as concerned with *what* they grow up to be career-wise as I am with *who* they grow up to be. I want them to become faithful wives and husbands, loving parents, brave believers, good friends, and committed citizens.

Being a *menschen* means living a life of integrity. "Integrity" comes from Latin words that when put together mean "untouched, whole, entire." In modern English, integrity means—

1. The quality or state of being complete; unbroken condition; wholeness; entirety

2. The quality or state of being of sound moral principle; uprightness, honesty, sincerity.

When we speak of living with integrity, then, I think of knowing exactly who you are and always being that person—not compartmentalizing, for instance, so that you are Cathy Christian on Sunday when you go to church but Betty Businessperson the rest of the week. I remember when Tripp held his first Promise Keepers meeting in Marin County in 1992. Since we had attended many churches, our circle of acquaintance was very large. Tripp invited all the men he knew from each church we had attended. At that first meeting, many men who knew each other in the business world were surprised to see each other there—because neither knew the other was a Christian.

There's something wrong there.

There's also something wrong when someone is too loud and pushy about his or her faith. We're to be salt and light. I take that to mean that somehow people see we're different. In our quiet confidence, our faith makes itself known.

The teen years are when this process of *menschen*-building, of learning to be salt and light, of learning to be in the world but not of it, all come together. For many years we've been making good decisions for our kids, explaining and, hopefully, thereby teaching them how we make those decisions. As they grow into the teen years, it's time for our kids to begin learning to live more independently, making their own choices.

Notice I didn't say anything about turning the reins over to them at a certain age. It's a process of our letting go little by little as we see our kids are ready to make good choices. Here's how the process was described by the Kansas City focus group:

Michael: Parents have a right to say no without a reason. Kids don't have the right to an explanation. However, it makes it a lot easier on the relationship if they can. Trust works both ways.

Jennifer: (a 20-something mentor) "Respect."

Michael: "Yeah, they should respect you enough not to just think the kid is an illogical, immature kid who can't make decisions, because the kid is going to make his or her own decisions eventually. If parents just help with decisions, then when kids get to the point where they're capable of making decisions, they won't make all the wrong ones and go crazy with the freedom."

Jennifer: "I think a lot of it has to do with the age of the kid. With a little child a parent can say, 'No, because I told you so, and that's that,' because you can't reason as much with a younger kid. But parents sometimes forget. I know my mom and I had this discussion when I was a senior in high school. My best friend got pregnant, and the first thing my mom said when that happened was 'Oh, I hope that never happens to you.' That hurt my feelings, and I said, 'Mom you've raised me. Why do you always assume just because I'm hanging out with somebody or just because I'm friends with someone that I'm going to make a bad decision?' To me it was a lack of respect, because it communicated that she still thinks of me as a little kid who can't make my own decisions. She apologized for that later, once I brought it to her attention. I do think as a child gets older and wants more freedom, the parent needs to communicate that he or she still has to keep boundaries, but I think that giving a reason shows respect, you know. So I think respect as the person gets older and giving him or her a little bit more freedom helps."

Jack: "At what point are you no longer a little kid?"

Jennifer: "When you leave for college. Actually, even after that."

Jack: "That's what I think, but, I mean, how does that apply?"

Jennifer: "I think each kid is different."

Michael: "I think it shouldn't be decided by age but that it should be based on maturity level. I guess it's the parent's job to judge what kind of decisions you think your kid would make. It comes down to trust also with that. You just have to talk to your kid and know your kid well enough to know what kind of decisions he or she would make in certain situations. At first, when there's a danger zone, you can say no. Eventually you can trust your kids enough so that when they're going into a shaky situation, you trust them enough to make that decision.

"And I guess it's a gradual thing from when you're a little kid and your parents are instilling values in you to getting older and developing a relationship with your parents to the point where it becomes more of a friendship and there's some accountability there. I know that once I graduate from high school or move out, my parents aren't going to be able to tell me what to do at all, but I still want to have that accountability with them even after I'm out of the house, because that's what I've had all through growing up. So you don't want that to just end. You shouldn't be building toward just letting your kids go and hoping they make a good life for themselves. You should be building toward a relationship with them and not just having it end when they leave. That would be pointless."

Matt: "I have a couple of things just to add to Michael's thoughts. If parents develop respect for their kids, when the kids go off to college, part of the reason they don't blow everything is because their parents respect them."

Is there risk involved during the process of turning the decision-making over to your teens? Yes, absolutely. And as discussed in the last chapter, just as grown-ups do, teens may make mistakes. That's why you still need to be a reliable part of their lives, so you can sense when they need a nudge to help them get back on track. The newest research indicates the teen brain, though intellectually impressive at test-taking, is still not fully mature until the age of 25. And specifically, teens' decision-making under stress is flawed. So there's no question about it: teens still need parents involved in their lives.

But increasingly as they mature, teens need to know their parents respect them and trust them to begin making decisions on their own. This is part of the process of learning to live a good life—not because your parents make you but because you choose to. This is learning to live with integrity.

Question: "Living with integrity"—what does this mean, practically speaking?

Matt: "I would have to say more than anything it means being true to what you feel and what you believe despite the consequences. I used to really struggle with this, because so many times it seems easier to let things go, and even unnecessary to stand up for what you're thinking or feeling. It's just been recently that I truly realized the impact integrity can have, often good, however bad the circumstances may appear.

"I kind of see it as a pool; some pools have leaks and can't hold water. A person who lives a life without integrity is like a pool with a leak—it may be invisible to everyone, but it can't hold to the test. How good is a pool that doesn't hold water? Many people walk around with a small crack that no one can see, but eventually, through trials and tribulations, the crack will get worse and worse, until the pool is empty.

"I think integrity can be built up and torn down. It's an ongoing project, and even after you build it up, you have to protect it from being torn back down."

Brandon: "Living with integrity means trying to stay true to the code of morals that you believe is right. In my case, I believe the rules that God has set down are the only true morals that should be kept. To live with this definition of integrity means trying to apply this set of morals to every avenue of life."

Brittany: "Practically speaking, I would say integrity means doing what you commit yourself to doing. An awesome example of integrity is a family at my church. If they say they're going to do something, they do it right away. If they say they'll give you something—for example, a recipe—it's there the next time you see them. It's so easy to forget the little things like this, but they don't—and it shows. You know you can trust them with the important things. They're probably the only people besides my family I would trust with my life.

"On a deeper level, I would say integrity includes following through with the standards you set on God's Word. Having them based on God's Word is the key."

Nathan: "Practically speaking, it means to live by your morals no matter how hard it gets."

Kristen: "Living with integrity is so important in the modern, cynical world. If non-Christians see believers without integrity, it leads them to resent Christianity as a whole. I think living with integrity means practicing what you preach, not being a hypocrite. Integrity means being the same on the outside as on the inside, consistent throughout."

Christian teens trying to live with integrity face many challenges. Most obvious are the challenges from unbelieving students and teachers. My son, Zach, who at 16 became a National Merit Finalist—we call him "the brainiac"—is challenged by other superintelligent students with remarks like "How can you be a Christian? I thought you were smart!"

In Australia, people speak of the "tall poppy syndrome"—that is, when someone excels, he or she becomes a target, more vulnerable to being cut down. The tendency of Australians to put down and humiliate those who stand out in public life has become a much-debated and debilitating problem for the nation.

We have some of that same spirit in North America—only here it has to do with moral character. For those without a strong code of morality, a person whose life is upright and pure will always present a challenge. I see it again and again as my children are growing up. When other kids find out they've made promises to remain pure, they do their best to tempt them away from that promise.

Discussion Starters

The following movies are great starting points for talking about maintaining integrity through difficulties—as well as how easy it is to throw it all away.

Quiz Show, 1998, John Turturro, Ralph Fiennes
This thought-provoking movie is based on the true story of the corruption of a well-bred and gifted young man, Charles Van Doren, who competed for the championship on the once-popular TV show *Twenty One.* The story of his moral failure and the resulting scandal shows just how effortless the slide into corruption can be. Rated PG

Eight Men Out, 1988, John Cusack
Another true story—this time of the 1919 Chicago White Sox, eight of whom accepted a bribe to throw the World Series, and one who refused but whose sin was failing to expose what he knew was wrong. Rated PG

Finder's Fee, 2001, James Earl Jones, Eric Palladino
This movie, about a young man who finds a lottery ticket and finds out it's a winner, demonstrates how vulnerable even a nice guy is to temptation and shows how giving in once can swiftly snowball into a larger-than-life series of sins. Rated R for language—no sex and only one not-too-bad violent act. A true cautionary tale to watch with your teen.

Question: What difficulties do you face each day from your peers and your teachers?

Joel: "From my peers I'm mainly challenged for what I do or how I act. If I act like a Christian, I follow the rules too much. It's quite annoying to get that intimidation. Teachers are difficult in how they stress their liberal views."

Sarah: "Kids ask me sarcastically if I'm perfect, and they ridicule me for actually wanting to remain a virgin until marriage.

"I've been made to stand out in the classroom by a teacher because of what I believe. In a class discussion in health class we had to share and discuss what the first priority in our lives was. I was the only one who said my top priority was God."

Brandon: "My friends see my faith as a type of oddity. I don't believe they understand the full scope of what a relationship with Christ means. They think it is an oppressive, intolerant belief system that has gotten lost in the crowd of other more modern and accepting belief systems. I believe that they think it's outdated.

"I've struggled during my four years in high school by being known as one of the few conservative, Christian students. I feel much more confident in that role now, but at times, especially in the beginning of high school, it was a bit intimidating and lonely at times. Many teachers, especially in the honors classes, allow for open debate on almost every subject, and often I was the sole person on the conservative side of any issue, whether it was about politics, sex, history, or religion. My mom felt that these constant debates were counterproductive and that the teacher should have made an effort to make them more balanced. One thing it did make me do was become more informed on the issues and know better how to argue them!"

Alyse: "Non-Christian peers challenge me every day because they may ask questions about Christianity that I sometimes can't answer. I also try to behave the best way possible around them, because I know that the best missionary tool is to show them I have something special that they don't have."

Conflict between our Christian values and the world we live in is inevitable. Christian teens know they can expect it, and though it hurts, they understand. They're dealing with people who don't know the grace and redemption they've come to know through Jesus Christ.

But there's something sincere Christian teens have to deal

with that's even more difficult—and that's insincere Christian teens.

In the last chapter, I mentioned that our family had been living in Marin County, California, a place that's very hostile to Christianity and where only four percent of the population attends church. Anxious to move to a more Christian culture, we ended up in northern Virginia, where we felt like kids in a candy store—churches on every corner, Christian principals and teachers and doctors, a seemingly unified moral code.

At first our teens came home with glowing reports from public school about how much easier it was to fit in here, since it seemed the majority of students were Christian. We started going to the denominational church that seemed to attract the most students from the high school. It was the kind of church where teens met and worshiped in one place, little children in another, and adults in a third. So Tripp and I dutifully dropped off our kids and went to church together.

But it wasn't long before—as my kids would put it—there was a disturbance in the force, meaning something happened to stir up the tranquility of Sunday morning. My kids, brought up in a place where Christians stood out as different—not in an unattractive way, but still different—were shocked to see kids at the Sunday morning youth group whose behavior at school was far from what they would have expected from Christians.

"Christian" girls from the church dressed immodestly at school and at church as well. Kids went outside to smoke. Some chattered incessantly, even during the sermon, which was delivered by the youth pastor to make it more appealing.

I saw the lack of respect when some teens came to "big church." They didn't sit with their parents but in teenage clumps, passing notes, giggling, seeming not to care if their behavior was disruptive to those around them.

Question: What problems do you have with Christian peers? How do you handle them?

Kristen: "Sometimes you have to be around people who are doing the wrong things. My roommate (I'm a freshman in college) is a heavy drinker, smoker, and all-around partier. She cusses constantly. She does, however, claim to be a Christian. At first I'll admit I preached to her some, but then I realized it wouldn't help any. So now I treat her with love instead of disdain. Remember to love people first before you try to reform them. It doesn't work the other way around. People don't respond to your looking down on them.

"It gets really tough when your Christian friends start going wild. I'm at a loss for what to do about that. You can't 'call them out' and accuse them of being a bad person. I have a friend who does that, and nobody wants to be around her anymore. But sometimes it's necessary to confront people. Other times you'll want to get help from people who know better what they're doing and have more experience. It can really be a big help, too, to get a Christian adult who has previously been involved in a dangerous lifestyle to talk to you about how to help your friend or maybe talk directly to your friend. I'm going to have to confront one of my friends soon who has taken up serious drinking since she went to college, and I don't know what to say yet, but I know God will give me the right words."

Brandon: "It really depends on the situation. I don't try to right every wrong I see. Sometimes, people—teenagers especially—don't respond to advice, but rather experience. No matter how much you tell them something is wrong, it takes firsthand experience to realize the consequences of one's actions, and throughout this whole time it can hurt to watch it happen."

Matt: "I have a Christian friend right now in just this situation. I try to be as supportive as I can without compromising my integrity. It's difficult, because you want to help, but you have to be sure not to judge as well. I definitely wouldn't walk away, and as far as getting help, it really depends on the severity of the situation. You don't want to lose your friend's trust, but if it escalates, you have to get help, because worse than losing your friend's trust is losing your friend.

"How I handle situations depends on the person. A lot of times I don't really preach; I just try to stand firm to my beliefs and hope my actions reach them. Often it doesn't really do any good to harp on it, especially people who are drinking. I think it was Charles Finney who said it doesn't do any good to lead those who aren't 'in the right state of mind' to Christ. I try not to get into situations where this is truly a problem."

When the prom and then homecoming took center stage in our community in 2004, some of the church parents seemed offended by our family's public position against freak dancing. That was hard for me to figure out. Either they felt guilty because it had been going on for years, and it took a newcomer to draw attention to the proverbial elephant in the living room, or like their kids, they wanted to blend in with the rest of the community.

Question: Do you attend school dances? Why or why not? Would your parents approve of what goes on there? How do you feel about it yourself?

Alyse: "I attended one homecoming and one prom. I had a great time, but I did not approve of some of the dancing going on there. I enjoyed the prom more because the lights were on and the people there behaved much better. I went only because my boyfriend at the time wanted to go. My parents would not approve of the behavior of the majority of the teens. Luckily, I went there with better-behaving teens. Besides dancing inappropriately, there were clearly drunks there. I caught sight of a few couples making out in the corners, and I would never wear a dress like some of the ones I saw there."

Brandon: "I used to, but then I realized there really is no point in going. More than half the kids freak dance, and I really don't need to see or be around that. I can't dance even as it is, unless it's swing or ballroom dancing, and that's considered outdated or old-school. My parents would definitely not approve of a lot of what goes on at school dances, but that doesn't mean there aren't kids who go to dances who go to have a fun, clean time. I have friends who do this all the time. However, there are so many other things I would rather be doing than being at a school dance. I really just don't need the temptation of being around those dances and the baggage that comes with it."

Unidentified teen: "Our only school dance was the prom, and I went just to get dressed up and all that. But really, teens' dancing, if you can even call it that, is a giant clothed orgy. The guys do it to get turned on; the girls do it to feel sexy and in control. As one of my teachers put it, 'If there were dogs in my yard doing what you people do at prom, I would turn the water hose on them.' I danced that way for two songs at a dance once, and I felt so miserable afterward that I promised myself I would never do it again. I kept wondering what the guys must think of me, and it made me focus on my sexuality for a long time even after the dance was over. It's not a positive activity in any respect."

The school dance issue is a good illustration of the kind of decision-making we should be turning over to our teens, though we would certainly want to be available to discuss their thoughts as they make up their minds. It would be counterproductive to forbid them to go to the dance because of the bad behavior of others.

The fact that freak dancing was tolerated by the principal, teachers, and chaperones at our local school for years is sad, because there were so many missed opportunities to teach kids appropriate behavior, good judgment, consideration of others, self-respect, and just plain good manners.

But how the teens handled it was up to each of them individually. Some chose not to attend the dances. Some chose to attend and maintain their own standards. Some attended and bowed to peer pressure to act in a way they later regretted. An extraordinary leader, Christian, took action and worked to right the situation through the civic options available—in this case rounding up a delegation to approach the school board for change.

What Does God Say?

Here is what God tells us about integrity:

> *Blessed is the man who does not walk in the counsel of the wicked or stand in the way of sinners or sit in the seat of mockers. But his delight is in the law of the LORD, and on his law he meditates day and night. He is like a tree planted by streams of water, which yields its fruit in season and whose leaf does not wither. Whatever he does prospers (Ps. 1:1-3).*

Question: How have your parents prepared you to live with integrity? What more could they have done?

Unidentified teen: "My parents prepared me to live with integrity by giving me standards to follow and enforcing them and instilling in me a desire to live for Christ. Something I feel they could have done better is to let me make more of my own choices. Their rules were very strict and left little room for me to make decisions of my own. This presents a problem when I'm out in the real world without their guidance and I have no one enforcing the rules. The freedom is so enticing. I wonder if it would have been easier to go through this while I was at home with their talking through my mistakes with me and encouraging me to make the right choices next time."

Brandon: "My parents have taught me to walk with integrity through their example. I've watched them apply God's goals to their lives and have noticed the results."

Kristen: "Integrity has to be modeled, not taught. My parents live with integrity, and that's how I learned to be a woman of integrity. Kids and teenagers are perceptive—they know what their parents are doing even if they're not told. Be a person of integrity and surround your children with role models of integrity, and they'll learn to develop integrity too."

Especially during the teen years, it's important for parents to teach their teens to think positively and constructively, to steer them away from feelings of victimization and blame, and to draw their attention to role models or heroes who live lives of integrity.

Taking up for your teen when he or she is wrong, as with the man who begged that his daughter still be allowed to participate in team sports after driving drunk, will cripple your teen. No matter how much it hurts to see your teen unhappy, he or she needs the experience of dealing with the consequences of poor behavior.

I teach my kids that every moment matters. Life is filled with some big choices. *Will I go to college? How will I earn a living? Who will I marry? Where will we live?* But character is revealed in the smallest details of their lives, moment by moment, as they make decisions that will bring their character more in conformance with Christ's. Each small decision builds on another, bringing them closer or taking them farther away from God. Impress this on your children's hearts: each decision matters. They'll find that as they surrender their lives, God will draw them closer. He'll draw them closer even as He gives them everything they need—strength, courage, wisdom, hope—to live a life of integrity.

✳ ✳ ✳

May God richly bless you and your family
as you journey together through the teen years.
May He bless each day and every lesson.
May he bless your relationship and your conversation.
May your home be filled with the laughter and tears
that come from honest communication—
straight from their hearts to yours,
and your heart to theirs.